The Seven Streams of the River Ota

Directed by Robert Lepage
Conceived by Éric Bernier, Normand Bissonnette, Rebecca
Blankenship, Marie Brassard, Anne-Marie Cadieux,
Normand Daneau, Richard Fréchette, Marie Gignac,
Patrick Goyette, Ghislaine Vincent, Macha Limonchik,
Gérard Bibeau and Robert Lepage
With an introduction and commentary by Karen Fricker

Early one August morning in 1945, several kilos of uranium
was dropped over Japan and changed the course of human
history. Fifty years later, Hiroshima's vitality is striking: the
city where survival itself seemed unimaginable, today
incarnates the notion of renaissance.

The Seven Streams of the River Ota makes Hiroshima a literal
and metaphoric site for a theatrical journey through the last
half-century. In *The Seven Streams*, Hiroshima is a mirror in
which seeming opposites – East and West, tragedy and
comedy, male and female, life and death – are revealed as
reflections of the same reality.

Collaboratively developed over three years and now
complete in seven sections, *The Seven Streams* is the first of
Robert Lepage's ensemble creations to be published.

'Ravishingly beautiful . . . completely compelling, full of
emotional and imaginative richness and a deep, mysterious
feeling for the very pulse of twentieth-century living.'
Scotland on Sunday

'Of all Lepage's magic boxes, this is the masterpiece.'
Independent on Sunday

'Nothing you've ever read or seen has prepared you for
Robert Lepage's new play . . . *The River Ota*'s enduring
astoni   io Lepage
explo   ig but of
love.'

'A magnificent spectacle, the opus of one of the international theatre community's true creative geniuses.' *Japan Times*

'An exceptional theatre event which invents itself in front of and with those who are witnessing it; a theatre of courage and lucidity, indispensible and reinvigorating.' *Le Monde*

'With *The Seven Streams* Lepage has succeeded like never before in marrying aesthetics and emotion – the whole gamut of emotions . . . Everyone should see this monument one time in their life.' *La Presse*

'Robert Lepage and his collaborators have given themselves a task that is as immense as it is deeply needed. They seek to create a theatre where the terrifying and incomprehensible reality of our time is inseparably linked to the insignificant details of our everyday lives – details that are so important to us, so trivial for others. For this, they are experimenting with a theatrical language where today's technology can both serve and sustain the humanity of a live performance. What a splendid task! What heroic ambition!' Peter Brook

The Seven Streams of the River Ota

by Éric Bernier, Normand Bissonnette, Rebecca Blankenship, Marie Brassard, Anne-Marie Cadieux, Normand Daneau, Richard Fréchette, Marie Gignac, Patrick Goyette, Ghislaine Vincent, Macha Limonchik, Gérard Bibeau and Robert Lepage

with an introduction and commentary by Karen Fricker

Methuen Drama

Methuen Modern PLays

First published in Great Britain in 1996
by Methuen Drama
Methuen Publishing Ltd
215 Vauxhall Bridge Road
London SW1V 1EJ

www.methuen.co.uk

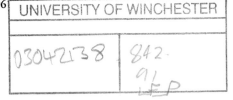

ISBN 0 413 71370 9

Methuen Publishing Ltd reg. number 3543167

A CIP catalogue record for this book is available at the British Library

Typeset by Wilmaset Ltd, Wirral
Transferred to digital printing 2002

Introduction

Like so many of Robert Lepage's works, *The Seven Streams of the River Ota* is a project defined by paradox. It was a paradox that inspired the piece: on his first trip to Hiroshima, expecting to find devastation, Lepage instead discovered a place full of vitality and sensuality. He was so struck by Hiroshima that he decided to create a production that took the city's unexpected liveliness as its jumping-off point.

A creative team was assembled, and rehearsals began in Quebec City in January 1994. Lepage knew he wanted to create the production collaboratively, drawing together genres beyond the traditional theatrical media of text and performance. He knew he wanted it to be international – not just in the venues it would play, but in the make-up of the company, in the subject matter, and in the way it treated language. He knew he wanted it to be epic in scope. Beyond that, little else was known; all the usual 'givens' of theatre – text, plot, characters, venue, end date – were conspicuously absent.

In traditional theatre environments, the script is the catalyst for production, whereas the physical setting is among the last elements to be folded into the creative process. *The Seven Streams* reversed this pattern: the set was one of the first things to be finished about the show, and that wooden rectangle became a literal framework for a production that reinvented itself constantly over the three years of its life. The collaborators created the show through a cyclical process of brainstorming, improvisation, discussion, and structuring, making changes throughout the process, and setting down the text only in the final days before performance. As the production developed into three distinct versions – three, five, and eight hours long – whole plot lines were developed, explored, and changed; characters added and dropped; and playing orders shifted.

What remained constant was the production's

preoccupation with mirror images: East and West; male and female; devastation and rebirth; photography, and the images it captures; theatre, and the life it recreates. Rather than reveling in difference, the production demonstrates and celebrates the necessary – and paradoxical – co-existence of opposites.

Whereas in traditional theatre the author's role decreases considerably once the script has been handed to the actors, in this production the actors *are* the authors, and this fact informs both their extraordinary openness to changes in the show, and the uniquely alive quality of their performances. As someone who has observed *The Seven Streams'* progress since its inception, I never stop being surprised by the freedom with which the company plays with the production, calling into question small details and major elements at every stage of the process.

This is not to say that they are cavalier with change – every shift is pondered, discussed, and agreed upon before it's executed – but it is clear that the group has created an atmosphere that not only allows them, but requires them, to take risks. The company is loath to take individual credit for lines, characters, and ideas; to their minds, an ensemble created this show, which over time has acquired a life of its own, and yet remains completely theirs. And it is their ability to give up control over the show that has made their ownership of it so complete.

The notion of publishing the text of this production is, appropriately enough, a paradoxical one. *The Seven Streams* comes to life on stage through a seamless blending of text, staging, and performance; to attempt a full and accurate description of the production, I have included here extended commentary on the physical performance in the place of stage directions.

As photography is an important element of *The Seven Streams*, it seems appropriate to think of this script as a snapshot of *The River Ota* at a certain point in its history – specifically, as it was performed in Vienna in June 1996. The river will have flowed on, and doubtless there will be changes both major and minor in the production by the time this script sees print.

Karen Fricker
July 1996

Note about translation: Many portions of this production are performed in languages other than English. To retain the production's multi-lingual quality, we have included these portions both in their original language and in English translation. The stage directions are included in the English versions, and we have placed ellipses (. . .) in the original language where the stage directions would fall.

Production History

Version 1 (three hours)

Edinburgh International Festival	August 1994
Manchester '94 – City of Drama	October 1994
The Tramway, Glasgow	October 1994
Riverside Studios, London	October 1994
Maison des Arts de Créteil – Festival d'Automne à Paris	November 1994

Version 2 (five hours)

Wiener Festwochen, Vienna	May–June 1995
Theaterformen '95, Braunschweig, Germany	June 1995
Spoleto Festival, Spoleto, Italy	June–July 1995
Festival d'Estiu de Barcelona GREC – Ajuntament de Barcelona	July 1995
Präsidialabteilung der Stadt Zürich – Zuercher Theater Spektakel	August 1995
Aarhus Festuge, Aarhus, Denmark	September 1995
Tokyo Bunkamura, Tokyo	October 1995
Harbourfront Centre, Toronto	November 1995
Kampnagel, Hamburg	December 1995

Version 3 (eight hours)

Le Carrefour International de Théâtre de Québec	May 1996
Wiener Festwochen, Vienna	June 1996
Staatschauspiel Dresden, Germany	June 1996
Københaven '96, Copenhagen	August 1996
Ludwigsburger Scholssfestspiele, Ludwigsburg, Germany	September 1996
The Royal National Theatre, London	September–October 1996
Stockholm Stadsteater	October 1996
Maison des Arts de Créteil – Festival d'Automne à Paris	November 1996
The Brooklyn Academy of Music, New York	December 1996

This version of *The Seven Streams of the River Ota* was first performed at the Carrefour International de Théâtre de Québec in Quebec City on 17 May 1996. It subsequently played, in an altered form, in Vienna, Dresden, Copenhagen, Ludwigsburg, London, Stockholm, Paris, and New York. The text printed here reflects the production as it was presented in Vienna, in which the cast and the order of playing were as follows:

Prologue
Jana Čapek   Ghislaine Vincent

1   Moving Pictures
Luke O'Connor   Normand Bissonnette
Nozomi Yamashita   Macha Limonchik
Nozomi's mother-in-law   Marie Brassard

2   Two Jeffreys
Karen, *the landlady*   Macha Limonchik
Jeffrey Yamashita (Jeffrey 2)   Normand Daneau
Nozomi's Mother-in-law   Marie Brassard
Jeffrey O'Connor (Jeffrey 1)   Normand Bissonnette
Luke O'Connor, *as an old man*   Richard Fréchette
Ada Weber   Rebecca Blankenship
The Sphinx   Richard Fréchette
Luke O'Connor   Normand Bissonnette
Kevin   Réjean Vallée
Tony   Michel F. Côté

3   A Wedding
Ada Weber   Rebecca Blankenship
The Librarian   Richard Fréchette
The Doctor   Marie Gignac
Jeffrey O'Connor   Normand Bissonnette
The Waiter   Réjean Vallée
Tourists   Marie Brassard
                                                        Michel F. Côté
                                                        Normand Daneau
                                                        Richard Fréchette
                                                        Ghislaine Vincent
                                                        Macha Limonchik

The roles of **Nozomi Yamashita, Karen, Sophie Maltais/La Môme Crevette**, and **Nathalie** were played in Quebec and Dresden by Macha Limonchik and in Copenhagen, Ludwigsburg, London, Stockholm, Paris, and New York by Anne-Marie Cadieux.

The roles of **Kevin, François-Xavier/Monsieur Petypon, Régis**, and **Pierre Maltais** were played in Quebec, Ludwigsburg, London, Stockholm, Paris, and New York by Éric Bernier and in Dresden and Copenhagen by Réjean Vallée.

The roles of **Luke O'Connor, Jeffrey O'Connor, The Interpreter, Étienne**, and the **German soldier** were played in Quebec, Ludwigsburg, London, Stockholm, Paris, and New York by Patrick Goyette and in Dresden and Copenhagen by Normand Bissonnette.

Directed by Robert Lepage
Assistants to the Director: Normand Daneau, Philippe Soldevila, Bruno Bazin, Alexandre Legault
Scenic design by Carl Fillion
Lighting design by Sonoyo Nishikawa
Costume and wig design by Marie-Chantale Vaillancourt and Yvan Gaudin
Image design by Jacques Collin and Éric Fauque
Music composed and performed by Michel F. Côté
Additional music by F. Poulenc, M. Miyagi, G. Puccini, A. Dvořák
Piano score by Claude Soucy
Puppets by Le Théâtre de Sable
Properties by Sylvie Courbron
Stage Manager: Éric Fauque
Sound Manager: Luc Désilets
Lighting Manager: Christian Gagnon
Chief Stagehand: Marc Provencher
Costume and Props Manager: Catherine Chagnon
Assistant to the Costumes and Props Manager: Cathy Lachance
Stagehands: Marco Olivier, Martin Lévesque
Technical Director: Richard Gravel

Tour Manager: Louise Roussel
Associate Producer, Europe: Richard Castelli – Epidemic
Associate Producer, United Kingdom: Michael Morris – Cultural Industry Ltd.
Associate Producer, North America: Menno Plukker
Producer: Michel Bernatchez

The Seven Streams of the River Ota was produced by Ex Machina in co-production with the Edinburgh International Festival; Manchester '94, City of Drama; La Maison des Arts de Créteil; Wiener Festwochen; Theaterformen '95, Braunschweig; Change Performing Arts, Milan; IMBE Barcelona; Präsidalabteilung Der Stadt Zürich, Zuercher Theater Spektakel; Aarhus Festuge; Bunkamura Tokyo; Harbourfront Centre, Toronto; Kampnagel, Hamburg; Les Productions d'Albert, Le Centre Culturel de Drumondville; Le Centre Culturel de l'Université de Sherbrooke; Les Productions Specta; Staatschauspiel Dresden; København '96; Ludwigsburger Scholssfestspiele; Stockholm Stadsteater; the Brooklyn Academy of Music, New York; Becks; and Cultural Industry Ltd.

THE SEVEN STREAMS OF THE RIVER OTA

Prologue: Iaido

The lights come up on the exterior of a Japanese house, which has a wooden porch and stairs leading down to a narrow raked stone garden. The house has seven sliding doors covered in rice paper.

A musician sits at the stage left corner of the rock garden behind a large percussion set. His live percussion and synthesizer music, as well as recorded music, accompanies the production.

Jana Čapek *enters. She is wearing a traditional blue kendo costume, carries a katana (Japanese sword), and has a shaved head. She walks to center stage and performs an iaido kata (martial arts exercise). She then addresses the audience.*

Jana   Iaido is a modern form of the ancient art of the samurai. These Japanese warriors practiced weaponry to overcome the enemy; but if you practice iaido today you don't have to measure up to someone else: the only adversary is yourself. To cut the ego with the sword is the ultimate combat. *The Seven Streams of the River Ota* is about people from different parts of the world who came to Hiroshima and found themselves confronted with their own devastation and their own enlightenment. For if Hiroshima is a city of death and destruction, it is also a city of rebirth and survival.

Jana *slides the three center doors open to reveal a screen, and exits.*

1: MOVING PICTURES
Hiroshima, 1945–46

1: The Torii of Miyajima

An image of the Torii (arch) of Miyajima is projected on the screen. Gagaku music plays. An American soldier and a Japanese boatman appear in silhouette behind the screen. The boatman helps the soldier put his gear – a duffel bag and a camera on a tripod – onto his boat and pushes off. The background image turns into running video of the Bay of Miyajima. The soldier holds up a light gauge, sets up his camera and shoots pictures. When the boat reaches a small dock, the boatman helps the soldier to alight.

The image of the dock fades away as an elderly woman in a kimono enters stage right and goes inside the house.

2: Hibakusha* 1

The American soldier, **Luke O'Connor***, enters, walking in the rock garden. An eerie, suspenseful sound accompanies his entrance. He wipes his face and opens his canteen, but it's empty. Through the doors of the house a woman sitting with her back to the audience is just visible, as is a white kimono, hanging up with its sleeves outstretched.*

Luke   Is anybody home?

Luke *takes a piece of paper out of his pocket and reads, in Japanese. He has a Southern US accent. His words are translated using supertitles.*

Luke   Luke O'Connor to iu Amerika-gun no cameraman de tatemono to shuhen no shashin wo totte imasu. Amerika-seifu ga genbaku no higaijo-kyo- no toukei wo tsukulu tameno shashin desu. Otaku no sotogawa to naka no shashin wo tolasete itadakitai. Tsulai de shouga nichibei lyoukoku ni

*A *hibakusha* is a survivor of the atomic bombs dropped on Japan during the Second World War.

totte jyu-yo- na koto nanodesu. [My name is Luke
O'Connor. The US Army has assigned me to take pictures of
houses and buildings and their surroundings to allow the
American government to make statistics of physical damages
that have been caused by the bomb. So I have to take some
pictures of the outside and inside of your house. I know it
may be painful for you, but it is very important for the army
and both of our countries.]

The elderly woman comes out of the house. They bow slightly. **Luke**
*puts his bags down and climbs the stairs, sets up his camera and points it
at the house.*

Luke   Would you please open the door, ma'am?

*She doesn't react. He moves towards the door. She takes a step to stop
him.*

Luke   Listen. I'm gonna have to get in there to take some
pictures. Do you understand? Pictures?

*She does not seem to understand. He reaches for one of the doors, but the
old woman blocks his way. She looks terrified.* **Luke** *backs off.*

Luke   All right. I'm just gonna take pictures of the outside
and the surroundings.

*He goes back to his camera, points it towards the audience. As he
measures the light, he becomes more aware of the heat.*

Luke   Could I get some water? Hot. Me. Water?

The woman behind the doors, **Nozomi,** *speaks the Japanese word for
'water'.*

Nozomi   Mizu.

Chimes play. **Luke** *gives his canteen to the elderly woman, who is*
Nozomi's Mother-in-law. Luke *speaks to her as she re-enters
the house.*

Luke   Thank you very much, ma'am, you're very kind.

Through the doors, **Nozomi** *speaks to him in English with a heavy
Japanese accent. Their dialogue is punctuated by soft chimes and
gongs.*

Nozomi   Light is very nice in the afternoon.

Luke   I'm sorry?

Nozomi   Light is very nice in the afternoon, but at night the sunset on the River Ota is beautiful. The sky becomes orange.

Luke   Oh! really . . .

Nozomi   Are you from New York?

Luke   No ma'am, I'm from Houston, Texas.

Nozomi   Houston is in the south, near the sea, isn't it?

Luke   Yes, it is. My God, how come you speak such good English?

Nozomi   My husband was a diplomat. He worked for Foreign Office. He teach me English.

Luke   Have you ever been to the United States?

Nozomi   No.

Luke   How come you know so much about America?

Nozomi   I read magazines.

Luke   What kind of magazines do you read?

Nozomi   Magazines from America.

Luke *laughs*.

Luke   What's your name?

Nozomi   Nozomi.

Luke   Listen, Nozomi, I'm really gonna have to get in there to take some pictures. Or else, I'm gonna get in trouble. Do you understand?

He half opens a door. **Nozomi** *closes it abruptly from the inside.*

Nozomi   No. Come Tuesday night. Mother-in-law, not here. I'll let you take pictures. Tuesday night.

Puzzled, **Luke** *folds up his camera, picks up his bags, and exits.*

The **Mother-in-law** *comes out of the house with his canteen, but*
Luke *is gone. She slides open the three center doors to reveal the opaque
screen, and goes inside the house. Blackout.*

3: Cheesecake

*An American soldier, carrying a paintbrush, is silhouetted against the
screen, which is tinted chartreuse. Music plays, a mixture of
synthesized French horns and percussion. The soldier begins to 'paint'
the screen with his brush. A photograph of an American military plane
from the 1940s emerges. The image turns into running video of the plane
flying. The soldier holds his hand up and the plane stops suddenly – the
film freezes in one frame. The soldier 'paints' the plane some more; the
film starts running again, and the plane flies off, nearly hitting him.*

*The soldier picks up a bucket and gestures at the plane, tossing paint at
the screen, which turns chartreuse again. He paints again, revealing
images of scantily clad women painted on the sides of planes. He throws
more paint at the screen, then paints an airplane taxiing down a
runway. He runs after it but can't catch up, and disappears stage right
as the plane takes off. Blackout.*

4: Hibakusha 2

*When the lights come up, the three center doors are opened to reveal the
inside of the house.* **Nozomi** *is sitting with her back to the audience in
front of the kimono, which we can now see is white with cranes stitched
in gold thread.*

Luke *enters with his camera over his shoulder. The same eerie sound
accompanies his entrance; again, gongs and chimes punctuate the
action.*

Luke   Good evening!

Nozomi   Oh! You came . . . How nice to have a visitor . . .
You arrive too late for sunset.

Luke   Yes . . . I'm afraid so . . . May I come in?

Nozomi   Yes.

He puts his bags down and climbs the stairs to the porch.

Nozomi   Your shoes!

Luke   Oh! I'm sorry.

He sits on the step and takes off his shoes.

Nozomi   The night is beautiful.

Luke   Sure is! I'm usually off duty in the evening, but tonight's an exception.

Nozomi   Do you want cigarette?

Luke   Sure.

She holds out a cigarette which he takes. He is still behind her. As he flicks his lighter open, she holds out her own cigarette. He then walks in front of her to light it, turning so he is facing the audience. He leans down to her. When he sees her face by the flame of his lighter, his expression turns to shock, and he stops moving. She takes his hand and lights her cigarette with his lighter. Pause.

Nozomi   Surprising, isn't it?

Luke   Yes it is . . . (*Pause.*) I brought you a little something.

He hands her a magazine.

Nozomi (*excited*)   Oh! *Life* magazine!

Luke   Yes. There were some around at the base, so I thought you might enjoy reading them.

Nozomi   Thank you very much. Very nice. Very kind. (*She bows a few times.*)

Luke (*ill at ease, he looks around the room*)   That's a beautiful kimono you got there . . .

Nozomi   It's my wedding kimono. It is made with real gold.

Uncomfortable, he goes out to the porch and lights his cigarette.

Nozomi   Are you married?

Luke   Yes I am.

Nozomi   Do you have photo of your wife?

He hesitates, then takes a picture out of his wallet.

Luke   Here's my wife.

Nozomi   Very pretty, very nice.

Luke   And that's my boy. (*He gives her another picture.*) His name is Jeffrey.

Nozomi   Jeffrey?

Luke   You like that name?

Nozomi   Yes. How old is he?

Luke   He's five. I miss him very much. You see, I've been out in the Pacific for the past two years, so I haven't seen him in a long time. (*She gives him back the photographs.*) Well, I'd better take my picture now.

He puts the camera just inside the entrance and takes two pictures of the inside of the house.

Luke   That's it, thank you.

He goes to leave and puts on his shoes.

Nozomi   That's all? I'm disappointed. I thought you take a picture of me.

Luke   No ma'am, I only have to take pictures of the inside and the surroundings.

Nozomi   Please . . . I thought you took pictures of physical damages.

He picks up his bags and exits. Blackout.

5: The train

Actual footage of the Japanese countryside, filmed through the windows of a train in motion, is projected on the full width of the screen, turning the front porch of the house into the inside of a moving train. The filmed images are tinted blue. Rhythmic percussion that sounds like a train plays. Three soldiers – one of whom is **Luke** *– are sitting stage left, having a raucous conversation; two other military personnel sit* *stage right. All are sitting in trap doors in front of the screens so that their upper bodies are silhouetted against the screen.*

Luke *and one of the GIs get into a fistfight; they are restrained by the other soldier.* **Luke** *opens one of the screens a few inches as if opening a window and leans against it, smoking a cigarette. The blue tint disappears from the video. The other characters slowly slip down the traps.* **Luke** *sits down and falls asleep. A red tint seeps into the video and the sound of flames crackling mixes with the train music. Blackout.*

6: Hibakusha 3

When the lights come up, we are back in the house and **Luke** *is photographing* **Nozomi**, *who is standing up wearing her wedding kimono. Her back is still to the audience.*

Nozomi I'm very tired . . . Must sit down . . .

He puts his arms around her and helps her sit down.

Luke (*relaxed*) Are you gonna be all right? Let's take a break. You want some sake? (*On the tatamis sits a tray with a bottle of sake. He hands her a glass.*) I'm starting to get used to this drink. Back home, I usually drink beer. That's my drink.

Nozomi Oh . . . we drink beer too. But it is more a man's drink. Women, they drink sake. What women drink in America?

Luke I don't know . . . Shirley Temples? (*He laughs.*)

Nozomi What is Shirley Temples?

Luke It's a drink without alcohol that was named after the actress.

Nozomi Oh! I see.

They drink a toast.

Nozomi Kampai.

Luke Kampai.

Nozomi I have a gift for your son . . . over there. (*She points stage right.*)

Luke   You really didn't have to.

He goes to pick up the gift. We see him in silhouette.

Nozomi   It is a wedding doll. A traditional doll we give to children . . .

Luke   Usually in America, boys don't play with dolls . . . They play with trucks.

Nozomi   He doesn't have to play with it . . . It brings good luck . . . It means someday he finds a good wife.

Luke   Oh well, in that case, thank you.

He comes back into view, holding the doll which is wearing a red kimono.

Nozomi   I'm ready for another picture now.

Luke   All right.

He puts the doll down and goes to help **Nozomi** *stand up.*

Nozomi   No. I'll stay here on tatami. (*She touches his face.*) What happened to your eye?

Luke   It's nothing. I just got into a brawl with a couple of GIs on my way to Nagasaki.

Nozomi   Who are these men?

Luke   They're part of a film crew. You know, they're doing a moving picture.

Nozomi   A Hollywood movie?

Luke (*laughs*)   No. They're doing a documentary on the reconstruction of Japan.

Nozomi   They film houses or they film people?

Luke   I don't know . . . (*Pause.*) Why do you want me to take a picture of you?

Nozomi   In Japan, at the funeral, we display a picture the person has chosen. I want to choose mine, but I only have pictures of me before bomb. After bomb, mother-in-law take no pictures, hide all mirrors. When I die, I want people to see my face.

Luke   I understand.

He adjusts her hair, and holds up the light meter to her face. She slips the kimono from her shoulders. **Luke** *freezes. She takes the meter from his hand, then takes his hand, and directs it to the nape of her neck and her back. She leans over and he caresses her.*

Nozomi   Close the door, please.

He slides the three doors closed; the audience sees their action now in silhouette. **Nozomi** *stands up, holds her hands out to him; he takes them. He goes to put his arms around her, but suddenly breaks away from her, opens one of the doors.*

Luke   I'm sorry, I just can't.

He goes to pack up his camera. He then sits down on the porch and puts on his shoes.

Nozomi   Is it your wife?

Luke   No, it's not.

Nozomi   Is it my ugliness?

Luke   No . . . It's mine.

He exits. Blackout.

7: Wedding pictures

The **Mother-in-law** *enters with a portfolio, puts it down on the porch, and kneels down to open it up. Dreamlike gong music plays throughout the scene. She takes out some photographs that have been half-destroyed by fire and looks at them sadly. She then slides open the three center doors to reveal the screen. One of the photographs she is looking at, of a Japanese wedding procession, appears on the screen. The image turns into running video; as the wedding procession comes closer the* **Mother-in-law** *stands and touches the groom's face, but the image disappears. A new video of the wedding ceremony plays. The* **Mother-in-law** *kneels in front of the screen. The bride and groom on screen clap their hands twice as part of the ceremony and hands clap* *offstage in synch with the video image, the* **Mother-in-law** *clapping with them. The scene freezes on the screen; the* **Mother-in-law** *stands up, cries out harshly, and slaps her hands against the screen several times; each time she slaps, the image grows smaller, until it's small enough for her to put her hands on it and 'drag' it into the portfolio, which she closes up and takes offstage.*

8: Hibakusha 4

Lights up outside and inside the house. **Nozomi**, *seated, and the* **Mother-in-law**, *standing, are visible behind the closed doors.* **Luke** *enters carrying his camera, bag, and a folder. He crosses the rock garden, then rushes to hide as he sees the* **Mother-in-law** *coming out with a handbag. She exits across the porch.*

Luke *goes to the porch, takes off his shoes, and goes to the open door, after making sure that the* **Mother-in-law** *is out of sight.*

Luke   Nozomi.

Nozomi   Luke-san . . . Come in! . . . I waited a long time.

He slides open the doors. The wedding doll is still sitting next to **Nozomi**.

Nozomi   I thought you would never come back . . .

Luke   I brought you what you've asked for.

Nozomi   Picture of me?

Luke   Yes.

He kneels in front of her, takes a photo out of the folder and gives it to her. She looks at it, then doubles over. He reaches out to her.

Nozomi   Please, leave me alone.

He persists and helps her to sit up.

Luke   I bought you a present.

He takes a lipstick out of his pocket and offers it to her. She doesn't move. He takes it out of its case and applies it to her lips. He kisses her; they embrace. Blackout.

A short pause. When the lights come up, they are lying asleep, half-undressed. **Luke** *caresses* **Nozomi**, *then stands up and gets dressed. He picks up the wedding doll, caresses* **Nozomi** *again, and kisses her naked shoulder and goes out onto the porch, shutting two of the doors behind him.*

Luke   I have to go now . . .

Nozomi   Will I see you again?

Luke   I don't know . . .

He puts his shoes on.

Nozomi   Thank you for picture.

As he is getting ready to leave, the **Mother-in-law** *comes in, sees him, hurries inside the house and shuts the door.* **Luke** *exits. Blackout.*

9: The doll

An image of a train goes across the screen; the train music from Scene 5 plays. Three soldiers including **Luke** *appear behind the screen, making giant silhouettes.* **Luke** *sits down with his head bowed. The wedding doll is on his lap, covered by a cloth. He slips off the cloth and the doll, facing away from* **Luke**, *slowly turns around and lifts its hands.* **Luke** *lifts his head. The doll moves towards* **Luke**'s *face and runs her hands down his profile. She goes to kiss* **Luke**'s *lips but keeps moving; her image disappears into* **Luke**'s.

Luke *stands up and turns towards the audience. A light comes on that illuminates him for a moment. Blackout.*

2: TWO JEFFREYS
New York, 1965

1: 'Who's on First'

The sliding doors are gone, replaced by three screens. On the left and right screens is projected a few minutes of Abbott and Costello's famous 'Who's on First' sequence with one of the comedians appearing on each screen. The center screen remains dark.

2: Karen's flat

Karen, *a woman in a loud plaid skirt suit and big glasses, tears down the center screen. She stands in a dingy bathroom with* **Jeffrey Yamashita** *('Jeffrey 2'), a young man with black hair and glasses. The bathroom is lit by a single overhead lightbulb with a pull-cord; the other two-thirds of the stage are still in darkness. Street noise is heard, as is the sound of drums and guitar music.*

Karen   So, this is the collective bathroom, which means you share it with everybody on the floor. Jesus Christ, it's really dirty! I would suggest, should you decide to rent the space, that you keep your personal belongings in your room and bring them with you if you need to use the bathroom. Because it's a really busy place, lots of people coming in and out of the building. So . . . if you don't want anybody to brush their dirty teeth with your toothbrush . . . you know what I mean, you follow? (*Pause.*) OK . . .

The first on the south side is occupied by a poet, whose actual name is William Dennison, but who insists on being called The Sphinx. He's into some kind of avant-garde . . . well . . . if you ask me après-garde, post-beatnik-mellow-cool-poetic-bullshit. Really stresses me out! Then there would be your room, and right across the hall live two young and cute guys named Kevin and Tony. They're a bit noisy, they're musicians, you know . . . as you can hear right now. I just have to tell you that because I have got this really busy schedule . . . I don't have any time to deal with complaints, all that type of bullshit. Oh, on the other side of the building lives a guy named Jeffrey. He's a really nice boy but . . . here . . . (*She beckons him to come closer.*) between you and me I think he's a hustler. So, I think I've covered it all. Oh! Do you have a cigarette?

Jeffrey 2   No. I'm sorry, I don't smoke.

He speaks with a stilted accent.

Karen   Oh! good for you! I just stopped smoking and I'm really stressed out. Where are you from?

Jeffrey 2   Japan.

Karen   Oh! you don't look Japanese to me.

Jeffrey 2   My father was an American.

Karen   Oh! you're a banana! . . . (*He looks at her blankly.*) White on the inside, yellow on the outside.

Jeffrey 2   No in fact, I'm quite the contrary. You see, I'm much more like an egg.

Karen   What do you mean?

Jeffrey 2   White on the outside and yellow . . .

Karen   Oh yeah, well, anyways, listen, I don't want to push anything on you. If you want it, call me. I'll leave you my card and we'll fix it over the phone, OK?

Jeffrey 2   If it is possible, I would like to take the apartment now.

Karen   Oh, good! First of the month is good for you?

Jeffrey 2   No, I would like to take the apartment now!

Karen   You mean now now-now? Like, right now, this moment?

Jeffrey 2   Yes.

Karen   Well, I guess it's feasible; it's empty right now. Listen, why not. I'll go down to my office and get the papers. I'll leave you here to feel the place out and I'll be right back.

Listen, I'm really happy you're renting the place. You'll be happy here. Bye bye.

She exits through the bathroom door, which is on the upstage side of the room. She leaves the door open; through it we can see a hallway, and, further upstage, a closed door.

Karen (*yelling*)   Kevin, Tony, can you turn it down, please. (*The drums and guitar music stop suddenly.*) Thank you.

Jeffrey 2 *looks around the bathroom, flushes the toilet, peers out the small square window on the stage left wall, the only window in the bathroom. He sits down on the edge of the bathtub, with his profile to the audience.*

Dreamy Japanese string music plays. The door in the hallway opens and **Tony**, *wearing a tank-top, enters with shaving gear, shuts the door, stands at the sink, turns on the tap, and starts to shave. He and the other characters who subsequently enter are oblivious to* **Jeffrey 2**'s *presence; the scene takes place in* **Jeffrey 2**'s *imagination.*

The Sphinx *enters, wearing a dark suit, turtleneck, and sunglasses and carrying a newspaper. He shuts the door, drops his trousers and boxer shorts, sits down on the toilet, and starts to read.*

Kevin *enters, with sunglasses on, his arm tied off with a length of rubber cord, carrying a tambourine. He shuts the door, sits on the upstage right edge of the tub, takes a packet of white powder and a syringe out of the tambourine and prepares a fix.*

Jeffrey O'Connor (*'Jeffrey 1', the same actor who played* **Luke**) *enters with a towel around his waist. He locks the door behind him, takes off the towel, and climbs into the tub.*

Jeffrey 2 *stands, turns towards the audience, reaches up and pulls the light-cord. Blackout.*

3: Japan 1

The music from the previous scene continues. The lower half of the stage left screen is illuminated. In silhouette, we see **Nozomi** *lying down behind the screen with her knees elevated. The* **Mother-in-law** *comes out onto the dimly-lit porch with a basin of water. As she* *tosses the water onto the rocks in the garden, we see that the water and her hands are bloody. She goes back inside and* **Nozomi** *hands a swaddled baby to her. The* **Mother-in-law** *comes outside carrying the baby; puts the baby down behind the stage right screen, and exits. Blackout.*

4: Two Jeffreys

Lights up behind the screens stage right and left. **Jeffrey 1** *pulls the screen from the stage left frame, and* **Jeffrey 2** *from the stage right frame.* **Jeffrey 1**'s *room is set back from the frame of the house; we see into it through a window. Outside the window is a fire escape ladder and a small ledge. Now, and whenever* **Jeffrey 1**'s *room is illuminated, a TV can be seen and heard through his window, and city sounds can be heard as well.*

Jeffrey 1, *who is leaning out of his window, shakes the screen as if it were a towel, then brings his head back inside. There is a man with white hair sitting in* **Jeffrey 1**'s *room with his back to the audience, watching TV.* **Jeffrey 1** *talks quietly to the older man as he gives him a sponge bath.*

Stage right, **Jeffrey 2** *is standing in his room, which is lit by a wall lamp. With the screen he's holding, he polishes a double bass, then leans it up against the back wall. He brings a music stand and bow on from offstage, then unpacks a small suitcase, arranging its contents – a baseball mitt, a Yankees cap, and a tea set – on a low table.*

Jeffrey 1 *climbs out on his ledge, lights a cigarette, and perches on the windowframe. He is wearing an unmatched track suit and tennis shoes.*

Jeffrey 2 *takes up his bass and starts to play.* **Jeffrey 1** *looks around trying to figure out where the sound is coming from. The older man starts coughing.* **Jeffrey 1** *climbs back into the apartment, covers the old man's shoulders with a blanket and shuts his window. Blackout.*

5: Band 1

Kevin *turns on the overhead light in the bathroom. He is carrying a tape recorder and microphone; he puts the tape recorder into the tub and* *paces around the bathroom reciting song lyrics.* **Tony** *enters carrying a snare drum. He shuts the door behind him, sits down on the toilet with the drum in front of him.*

Kevin   OK man, you ready? One, two . . .

Tony *starts to play his drum and* **Kevin** *talk-sings 'Mother Hudson'. The song has a beatnik, William S. Burroughs-esque quality.*

I want to hear the singing breast
Of women of earth
Receiving . . . juicy rivers . . .

I want to feel your juices
I want to slide real deep
I want to dive in your river
All the way to the bottom
Oh! my little river . . . Mother Hudson

I wish I could be a trout
And navigate your tunnel
That's the way I was born
And that's the way I want to die
Oh! my little river . . . Mother Hudson

Jeffrey 2, *wrapped in a sheet, clicks on his wall light and rubs his eyes.*

Kevin   Dee de dee de doo doo doo.

Jeffrey 2 *leaves his room and knocks on the bathroom door.* **Kevin** *and* **Tony** *stop playing, and* **Kevin**, *peeved, opens the door.*

Jeffrey 2   Hi! I'm sorry to interrupt you. But you see, I've been trying to sleep for the past three hours. I don't mind that you rehearse during the daytime. But at this time of the night, maybe you should concentrate . . . and work on the lyrics, maybe. (*Pause.*) Thank you very much.

Kevin   OK.

Jeffrey 2   Thank you. Thank you very much.

He gives several little bows, exits and goes back into his room.

Kevin   So, let's just tone it down bit.

Tony   OK.

They start playing and singing again, as loud as before.

Kevin
    I want to hear the singing breast
    Of women of earth
    Receiving . . . juicy rivers . . .

    I want to feel your juices
    I want to slide real deep
    I want to dive in your river
    All the way to the bottom
    Oh! my little river . . . Mother Hudson

    I wish I could be a trout
    And navigate your tunnel
    That's the way I was born
    And that's the way I want to die

    So let's roll along my love . . .
    My little river . . . Mother Hudson

Jeffrey 2 *starts to his door again, but changes his mind and clicks off his light.* **Jeffrey 1** *throws the door of the bathroom open, stalks in, yells 'hey!', grabs the light-cord, and pulls. Blackout.*

6: Spy 1

Lights up in the bathroom and **Jeffrey 1**'s *room.* **Jeffrey 2** *is standing at the sink with his shirt off, getting ready to shave;* **Jeffrey 1** *is on the ledge talking on the phone; the TV, as ever, is on in his room.* **Jeffrey 2** *catches sight of* **Jeffrey 1**'s *reflection in the mirror and goes over to the window to get a closer look.* **Jeffrey 1** *looks over and sees him;* **Jeffrey 2** *ducks out of the way.* **Jeffrey 1** *climbs inside and closes his window.* **Jeffrey 2** *climbs out the bathroom window onto the ladder, and peeks into* **Jeffrey 1**'s *window.* **The Sphinx** *comes into the bathroom carrying a newspaper, locks the door, drops his trousers and boxer shorts, and sits down on the toilet.* **Jeffrey 1** *opens his window and shakes a towel out the window, then shuts the window.*

Jeffrey 2 *quickly climbs back into the bathroom, feet first, turns, and does a take when he sees* **The Sphinx** *on the toilet.* **The Sphinx** *looks at him impassively.* **Jeffrey 2** *gathers his shaving gear together and tries to leave the bathroom, but the door is locked. He unlocks the door and leaves.* **The Sphinx** *stands up, re-locks the door, checks under the tub, and sits down again. Blackout.*

7: Japan 2

Lights up on the rock garden; dreamlike Japanese music plays. The **Mother-in-law** *is holding the hands of a little boy — represented by a puppet — and helping him to walk. She sits down on one of the steps of the porch with the child in her arms with her back to the audience and watches a little boat as it passes by. A model American aircraft-carrier passes by, heading in the other direction; the* **Mother-in-law** *gathers the child in her arms and hurries off stage right. Blackout.*

8: Spy 2

Lights up in the bathroom and in **Jeffrey 1**'s *room; in the bathroom,* **Jeffrey 2** *is taking a bath.* **Jeffrey 1** *opens the bathroom door.*

Jeffrey 1   Sorry . . . You should lock the door when you take a bath.

Jeffrey 1 *leaves the bathroom and goes to his room.*

Jeffrey 2 *gets out of the tub to lock the door, peeks out the window and sees* **Jeffrey 1** *buying drugs from a man — whose hands alone are visible.* **Jeffrey 1** *looks out his window, sees* **Jeffrey 2** *looking at him and storms out of his room.* **Jeffrey 2** *hurries to put on a towel.*

Jeffrey 1   (*knocks calmly first, then more aggressively*)   Open the door. Open the door. I want to talk to you. It's the third time I've seen you peeping into my apartment . . . What the fuck do you want?

Jeffrey 2 *cowers in the corner. Other people begin to shout back in the hallway — 'keep your voice down', 'what's going on', etc.*

Karen   OK OK OK . . . what's the problem here?

Jeffrey 1   I want to talk to the guy who's been peeping into my apartment!

Karen   What guy?

Jeffrey 1   The Japanese guy!

Karen   Tone it down . . . We're gonna deal with this in a civilized manner!

Jeffrey 1   Open the door or I'm gonna kick the shit out of you . . . !

Karen   No you're not, no you're not . . . (*She knocks at the door.*) Hey banana, open up . . . hello . . . don't be afraid, nothing will happen to you, we're just gonna have a talk. He's not gonna touch you . . . Jeffrey, tell him you're not gonna hurt him . . . Would you stop breaking my balls and tell him you're not gonna touch him?

Jeffrey 1   I'm not gonna touch him . . .

Karen   You heard that! He's not gonna touch you. Now get the hell out of there!

Jeffrey 2 *unlocks the door and comes out into the hallway.* **Tony** *is standing in his doorway;* **Karen** *appears in the bathroom doorway and talks to* **Jeffrey 2**.

Karen   Good boy, good boy, good . . . Now . . . Jeffrey says you were looking into his apartment . . . Were you or were you not?

Jeffrey 2 (*inaudible*)

Karen   I cannot hear you . . .

Jeffrey 2   Yes.

Karen   You see, an honest answer always comes out of an honest man. Now, what were you looking at?

Jeffrey 2   The World Series.

Karen   The poor kid is a baseball fan and he doesn't have a television!

Jeffrey 1 (*yelling*)   Am I supposed to believe that? Do you think I'm fuckin' stupid or what?

More shouting in the hallway ensues. **Jeffrey 2** *goes back into the bathroom and locks himself in.* **Jeffrey 1** *storms back into his room and shoves his TV right up to the window.*

Jeffrey 1   You want to watch TV? You're gonna get TV!

Blackout.

In **Jeffrey 1**'s *window, the TV plays an excerpt from a 1950s children's television program about nuclear awareness. The program is about the importance of knowing how to 'duck and cover' if the bomb drops.*

9: Ada's arrival

Lights up in the bathroom. **Jeffrey 1** *is standing at the sink washing a syringe.* **Karen** *and* **Ada**, *a tall young woman with long blonde hair, enter.*

Karen   Oh! Jeffrey.

Jeffrey *tries to hide what he's been up to.*

Jeffrey 1   I'm gonna be out in a few seconds.

Karen   Good, 'cause I have to show the place to Ada here. Jeffrey, Ada; Ada, Jeffrey.

(*To* **Ada**.) So, this is the collective bathroom, which means you share it with everybody on the floor. Jesus Christ, it's really dirty! I would suggest, should you decide to rent the space, that you keep your personal belongings in your room and bring them with you when you need to use the bathroom . . .

Jeffrey 1 *starts to leave.*

Karen   Oh! Oh! Oh! Jeffrey, can I talk to you afterwards for a moment?

Jeffrey 1   Well, I'm really busy, I gotta go.

Karen Well then, I'll talk to you now. Ada, would you be a nice little girl and step outside for a moment please? Thank you.

Karen *opens the door for* **Ada**, *who goes into the hallway.*

Karen So . . .

Jeffrey 1 What?

Karen So, do you have the rent money?

Jeffrey 1 No. I'm pretty broke right now . . . I'm gonna give you the money in three weeks.

Karen I'm giving you three days to find the money, otherwise you're out.

Jeffrey 1 I can't get the money in three days, just give me a week.

Karen It's always the same story. I mean, it's not my problem, you know. Find yourself a job. Rob a bank for Christ's sake.

Jeffrey 1 Shit, Karen, do you have to be so nasty?

Jeffrey 1 *storms out.*

Karen Sorry! . . . (*She leans into the hallway.*) Ada, can you step back in please? (**Ada** *does so.*) Thank you. (**Karen** *shuts the door.*) So what do you do? Are you a Swedish basketball player or something?

Ada Why?

Karen Well, you know, you're so tall and blonde and beautiful . . . just like me.

Ada My father was Dutch, and we're all like that.

Karen Ah! So that makes you a young Dutch. But the problem is . . . what we need here is a bit of Old Dutch to clean the place, you know Old Dutch to clean, you know . . . (*She gestures shaking cleanser.*) No you don't . . . So what do you do?

Ada I'm still a student.

Karen   Where do you study?

Ada   At the Manhattan School of Music.

Karen   And what are you studying?

Ada   Voice.

Karen   Oh! Good good good. OK, Ada. There's one last thing I wanna tell you. There's a fire escape right in front of your window, so I would suggest that you keep your window closed at all times. Good girl. I mean . . . this is New York. I don't want another murder on my conscience . . . Ha! Ha! Ha! That's a joke. (**Ada** *doesn't laugh.*) I'll be right out, OK?

Ada *leaves;* **Karen** *looks at herself in the mirror over the sink.*

Karen   Frightening!

She leaves. Blackout.

10: The camera

Lights up in both **Jeffreys'** *rooms.* **Jeffrey 2** *is playing scales on his bass;* **Jeffrey 1** *is holding a camera – the same camera* **Luke** *carried in 'Moving Pictures'.* **Jeffrey 2** *puts down the bow of his bass and starts to pluck the strings with his fingers.*

Jeffrey 1 *leaves his room and knocks at* **Jeffrey 2**'s *door.* **Jeffrey 2** *opens the door and jumps back, holding his bass between* **Jeffrey 1** *and himself.*

Jeffrey 1   Hi! Can we talk for a minute? I'm sorry about the other day. I guess, I just got carried away.

He holds out his hand.

Jeffrey 1   No hard feelings? (*They shake hands.*) By the way, my name is Jeffrey. What's your name?

Jeffrey 2   Jeffrey.

Jeffrey 1   No, no, no. That's my name. What's your name?

Jeffrey 2   My name is Jeffrey too.

Jeffrey 1   What do you mean? Your name is Jeffrey?

Jeffrey 2   Yes, my name is Jeffrey too.

Jeffrey 1   So, if you're Jeffrey two, then I'm Jeffrey one, 'cause I was here first.

Jeffrey 2   No, no . . . Who's on first.

Jeffrey 1   I'm askin' you, who is on first?

Jeffrey 2   That's the man's name!

Jeffrey 1   That's whose name?

Jeffrey 2   Yes.

Jeffrey 1   Well, go ahead, tell me!

Jeffrey 2   Who.

Jeffrey 1   The guy on first.

Jeffrey 2   Who.

Jeffrey 1   The first baseman.

Jeffrey 2   Who is on first.

Jeffrey 1   Have you got a first baseman on first?

Jeffrey 2   Certainly . . .

Jeffrey 1   Well, all I'm tryin' to find out is what's the guy's name on first base.

Jeffrey 2   Oh, no, no. What is on second base.

Jeffrey 1   I'm not askin' you who's on second.

Jeffrey 2   Who's on first.

Jeffrey 1   That's what I'm tryin' to find out.

Jeffrey 2   Well, don't change all the players around. (*They laugh.*)

Jeffrey 1   How come you know that? You get Abbott and Costello in Japan?

Jeffrey 2   No, but every serious baseball fan must know that.

Jeffrey 1   So you are a baseball fan!

Jeffrey 2   Yes, I used to play when I was a teenager.

Jeffrey 1   Whereabouts, in Tokyo?

Jeffrey 2   No, Hiroshima.

Jeffrey 1   You have a baseball team in Hiroshima? It must be a blast, eh? (**Jeffrey 2** *doesn't react*.) It's a joke . . . Listen, I'm trying to sell some of my stuff because I'm pretty broke right now. I got something here that I thought might interest you. (*He hands the camera to* **Jeffrey 2**.) This is a real antique. It belonged to my father. He was a photographer in the military. And he used this camera in Japan during the American occupation after the war. I can cut you a good deal on it.

Jeffrey 2   Why are you selling your father's camera?

Jeffrey 1   I told you I'm having some financial problems at the moment. You see, the landlady, she said that if I don't pay the rent today she's gonna evict me. (**Jeffrey 2** *doesn't understand*.) Throw me out.

Jeffrey 2   How much?

Jeffrey 1   Fifty.

Jeffrey 2   Forty.

Jeffrey 1   Forty-five. (**Jeffrey 2** *goes to hand the camera back to him*.) . . . All right, all right, forty.

Jeffrey 2 *takes some money out of his wallet, as if he is about to give it to* **Jeffrey 1**.

Jeffrey 2   If I give you the money, how do I know you don't buy the drugs?

Jeffrey 1 (*angrily*)   What I do with the money is my fucking business . . . Aw, just forget it.

He storms out, then comes back in.

Jeffrey 1   OK. My father is a very sick man, and, for reasons I don't want to get into, he can't get any medical care. So I buy morphine on the streets to give the old man a break.

Jeffrey 2   What's wrong with him?

Jeffrey 1   He has leukemia. Thirty-five and it's yours . . .
Now are you gonna take it? I'm not gonna give it to you.

Jeffrey 2 *gives* **Jeffrey 1** *some cash.* **Jeffrey 1** *goes to leave,
counting the money, then stops.*

Jeffrey 1   Wait a minute, you gave me fifty. (*He gives back a
few bills.* **Jeffrey 2** *resists.*) No, no, no, take it back. A deal is a
deal.

Jeffrey 2 *takes back the bills.* **Jeffrey 1** *leaves.* **Jeffrey 2** *sets up
the camera and points it toward the audience. The lights dim on the
scene in the apartment and come up on the porch. Japanese music plays.*

11: Japan 3

As **Jeffrey 2** *looks through the camera,* **Nozomi**, *in a white kimono,
slips onstage from stage right, directly in front of* **Jeffrey 2**.
Nozomi *sits down, then lies down, and rolls over several times, her
hands over her face, until she is lying face up on the stage right side of the
porch. The* **Mother-in-law** *enters carrying a tray. She covers*
Nozomi'*s face with a small white cloth. She picks up a frame and
removes* **Luke**'*s photo of* **Nozomi** *from it. She tears up the photo,
replaces it with another, of* **Nozomi** *on her wedding day, and puts the
frame by* **Nozomi**'*s head. She lights a stick of incense and a candle
and places them by* **Nozomi**'*s head.* **Nozomi** *remains lying on stage
throughout the next scenes. The* **Mother-in-law** *remains on stage
during the next scene.*

12: Photography lesson

Jeffrey 1 *clicks on the light in the bathroom; there is a red gel over the
bulb. He is there with* **Jeffrey 2**, *and various pieces of photographic
equipment are scattered about the room.*

Jeffrey 1   Now, the first thing you got to remember once
the paper is exposed is that there are four major steps: there's
the developer, the stop bath, the fixer and the wash. You got
that?

Jeffrey 2   The developer, the stop bath, the fixer, and the wash.

Jeffrey 1   Correct. Just take a look at the containers, I'm gonna run a little bit of water.

Jeffrey 2 *finds a photograph on the floor. He picks it up, smiling.*

Jeffrey 2   Is this a photo your father took?

Jeffrey 1   Yes.

Jeffrey 2   It's you here?

Jeffrey 1   Yes, that's me.

Jeffrey 2   How old were you?

Jeffrey 1   Six. That's a birthday party picture. You see that house in the corner . . . that was our house in Texas.

Jeffrey 2   That must be your mom?

Jeffrey 1   No, no, no. She's right over here. You see the woman in the black dress there . . . that's my mom . . .

Jeffrey 2   She's pretty! Is she still alive?

Jeffrey 1   Yes, yes, she still lives in Texas. My parents are divorced. What about yours? Are they still together?

Jeffrey 2 (*uncomfortable*)   No, my mother died ten years ago.

Jeffrey 1   Sorry. And what about your dad?

Jeffrey 2   My father left us when I was quite young.

Jeffrey 1   Whereabouts in Japan does he live?

Jeffrey 2   Oh, no, my father is an American.

Jeffrey 1   So you are an American?

Jeffrey 2   Well, I'm half-Japanese, half-American.

Jeffrey 1   Where does he live?

Jeffrey 2   Here, in New York City. But you see, I don't have much contact with him.

Jeffrey 1   Do you have your roll of film?

Jeffrey 2   Yes.

Jeffrey 1   We're gonna need total darkness for this.

Jeffrey 1 *clicks off the light.*

13: Luke's death

Lights up in the bathroom and in **Jeffrey 1**'s *room.* **Ada** *enters the bathroom with a bucket, rubber gloves, and a canister of Old Dutch cleanser, and starts to clean the bathroom.*

In his room, **Jeffrey 1** *talks to his father, tries to wake him up gently, then shakes him with increasing urgency. He rushes out of his room. We hear him pounding on* **Jeffrey 2**'s *door.*

Jeffrey 1   Jeffrey! Jeffrey, open up!

He rushes into the bathroom.

Jeffrey 1   Have you seen Jeffrey?

Ada   He left ten minutes ago.

He goes into his room, then returns to the bathroom.

Jeffrey 1   I'm sorry, my father has just passed away. I was wondering if you just could help me out.

Ada *takes off her gloves and goes with* **Jeffrey 1** *into his room. She opens the window, helps* **Jeffrey** *pick up his father's body and carry him to his bed, offstage. She covers the body with a sheet, finds* **Jeffrey**'s *phone, and calls an ambulance. She goes back into the bathroom, picks up the gloves, puts them down, and looks out the window.* **Jeffrey 1** *is leaning out his window, his head in his hands, sobbing.* **Ada** *goes into his room, gently pulls him away from the window, and embraces him. She shuts the window. Blackout.*

14: Band 2

Lights up in the bathroom. **Kevin** *and* **Tony** *are practicing again, and* **Jeffrey 2** *has joined their band with his bass.*

Kevin

    I want to feel your juices
    I want to slide real deep
    I want to dive in your river
    All the way to the bottom
    Oh! my little river . . . Mother Hudson

    I wish I could be a trout
    And navigate your tunnel
    That's the way I was born
    And that's the way I want to die
    Oh! my little river . . . Mother Hudson

Ada *opens the bathroom door.*

Ada   Listen, you guys. Could you just cool it? Jeffrey's father just died . . . So, just keep it down. All right? (*She exits.*)

Kevin   Well, let's tone it down a little bit . . . let's take it from the top . . . Jeffrey, you're a little bit off-key, so watch it, OK?

They start to play again, but **Jeffrey** *drops out and starts to leave.*

Kevin   What's wrong with you, Jeffrey?

Jeffrey 2   Didn't you hear? Jeffrey's father just died!

He leaves; the other two continue to play. **The Sphinx** *enters in his boxer shorts and, as ever, sunglasses. He clicks off the light.*

15: The suit

The lights come up in **Jeffrey 2**'*s room. He is sitting on the floor.* **Jeffrey 1** *knocks at the door.*

Jeffrey 2   Come in.

Jeffrey 1   Hi! . . . (*He's wearing a dress shirt and untied tie with his track suit bottoms. He looks at* **Jeffrey** *2.*) What's the matter?

Jeffrey 2   I heard about your father. I'm quite sad about that.

Jeffrey 1   No, no, no. It's all right. My father was very sick
. . . (*Pause.*) The funeral is this afternoon. I don't have a suit
to wear. I was wondering if you have anything dark or black
I could borrow.

Jeffrey 2   The only thing I have is my concert suit . . .

Jeffrey 1   Anything more formal than this would be fine.

Jeffrey 2 *goes offstage right and speaks from offstage.*

Jeffrey 2   Where's the funeral taking place?

Jeffrey 1   On Long Island. You know where that is?

Jeffrey 2   Yes.

He re-enters with a black suit on a hanger and gives the jacket to
Jeffrey 1, *who tries it on.*

Jeffrey 1   Look at this. We're almost the same size. It fits
perfectly.

Jeffrey 2   Yes . . . We could be brothers.

Jeffrey 1   Do you know how to . . . (*Gestures to the tie.*)

Jeffrey 2   Yes, sure.

He starts trying to knot the tie facing **Jeffrey 1** *and then stands behind*
him and puts his arms around his neck to knot the tie.

Jeffrey 1   That's fine. Don't get any wrong ideas.

Jeffrey 2   Don't worry. You're not my type. (*Pause.*) Is it
going to be a military funeral?

Jeffrey 1   No. My father was court-martialed for anti-
American activities. He spoke up against the nuclear tests in
the Pacific. Actually, he always thought that's where he got
cancer in the first place.

Jeffrey 2   Do you need someone to go to the funeral with
you?

Jeffrey 1   No, Ada is coming with me. It's gonna be a very
intimate ceremony. There's a reception afterwards. If you
want to come over, you're welcome.

Jeffrey 2   Sure.

Jeffrey 1   Thanks a lot. I owe you one. See you later.

Jeffrey 2 *hands him the trousers on a hanger.* **Jeffrey 1** *leaves.*

Jeffrey 2 *picks up his bass and starts to play. Blackout.*

16: The party

The Supremes' 'Stop in the Name of Love' plays as dim lights come up in all three rooms. There is a party going on; **Kevin, Tony, The Sphinx**, *and several women we have not seen before mill around from room to room, smoking and drinking.* **Jeffrey 1**, *quite tipsy, is on his ledge.* **Ada** *is leaning out of his window talking to him. She is wearing a dark suit.* **Jeffrey 2** *wanders around, drinking from a Japanese tea cup. He wanders into his own room, picks up his baseball glove and baseball and faces towards the audience. The Supremes fade out and the Japanese music fades in. The lights turn reddish in the apartment and come up on the porch, where* **Nozomi'***s body still lies.*

17: Japan 4

Jeffrey 2 *walks onto the porch and then into the rock garden; he turns to face* **Nozomi'***s body. The action in the party turns into slow motion. The* **Mother-in-law** *enters stage right on the porch, followed by* **Luke. Luke**, *dressed as in 'Moving Pictures' in his army uniform, kneels down next to* **Nozomi'***s body and lifts the cloth from her face. He replaces the cloth, picks up the picture frame and looks at the* **Mother-in-law**. *He then bows his head. The* **Mother-in-law** *gestures for him to leave. He gets up, and notices* **Jeffrey 2**. *He gestures for* **Jeffrey 2** *to throw him the ball. They play a few rounds of catch. The* **Mother-in-law** *moves towards* **Luke** *to make him stop and leave.* **Luke** *strokes* **Jeffrey 2'***s hair very gently, turns, and walks out, followed by the* **Mother-in-law**. **Jeffrey 2** *goes to* **Nozomi'***s body and blows out the candle. Blackout.*

18: Epilogue

The light over the bathroom sink comes on. **Jeffrey 2** *is in the bathtub.*
Jeffrey 1 *knocks at the door.*

Jeffrey 2   Yes?

Jeffrey 1   Jeffrey, it's Jeffrey.

Jeffrey 2   Just a second.

Jeffrey 1   I just want to say goodbye before you leave.

Jeffrey 2 *puts a towel around his waist and opens the door.*

Jeffrey 2   Hi!

Jeffrey 1   Hi! (*Gesturing to* **Jeffrey 2***'s state of undress.*) I'm
sorry about this. Like I said, I just want to say goodbye
before you leave because I won't be around this afternoon
and I don't wanna miss you.

Jeffrey 2   Oh! it's very nice of you, it's very kind.

Jeffrey 1   What time is your flight?

Jeffrey 2   At four o'clock. Before you leave, there's
something I would like to give you . . . Stay here. Just a
second. (*He scurries into his room, and scurries back with several
photographic plates in his hand.*) Here. These are photographic
plates that have never been developed.

Jeffrey 1   What are they pictures of?

Jeffrey 2   These are pictures of my father. I want you to
have them. It's a gift from me to you.

Jeffrey 1   That's very nice. Thank you. Bye.

Jeffrey 2   Bye.

Jeffrey 1   It was good to meet you. Take good care of
yourself. Good luck and . . . keep in touch!

Jeffrey 2   Yes. Promise.

They hug each other awkwardly. **Jeffrey 1** *exits and* **Jeffrey 2** *gets
back into the bath.*

The light over the sink fades out and the overhead light, with the red gel on, fades up. Live, percussive music plays.

A panel swings open in the upstage wall of the bathroom; **Ada** *and* **Jeffrey 1** *slip in.* **Jeffrey 1** *kisses* **Ada**. *He is developing* **Jeffrey 2**'s *plates. He dips a photograph into the bathtub, then reaches in and pulls out the plug.* **Jeffrey 2** *slips out of sight into the bathtub.*

Jeffrey 1 *rinses the photo in the sink, then takes the red gel off the bulb so that he and* **Ada** *can look at it. They both look at the photo with shocked expressions, then at each other.* **Jeffrey 1** *exits.* **Ada** *clicks off the bulb. Blackout.*

3: A WEDDING
Amsterdam, 1985

1: Red light 1

Four prostitutes in white lingerie and teased wigs rip the screens from the frames. The scene is lit by black light so that their lingerie and hair show up bright white, evoking Amsterdam's famous red-light district. Raucous music plays.

Ada *enters stage left, in a trenchcoat and carrying a shoulder bag, and seems to be scrutinizing the prostitutes. Slowly, panels filled with books slide on stage. By the time* **Ada** *reaches the stage right panel, the final wall of books slide into place and she plucks one from the shelf. The music fades out; a* **Librarian** *enters.*

2: The library

Ada   Excuse me sir. Do you speak English?

Librarian   Ya, a little bit.

Ada   I'm looking for a book by an American called Michael Osborne. It's on the Second World War.

Librarian   This whole department is about World War II. (*Pause.*) On what front? (**Ada** *looks at him quizzically.*) The Russian front . . . The Africa Corps . . . The Battle of Normandy . . . The London blitz . . . The Battle of the Pacific . . .

Ada   The Pacific.

Librarian   What event?

Ada   What do you mean?

Librarian   Pearl Harbor, Philippines, Guadalcanal?

Ada   Japan.

Librarian   Japan is a country, not an event. Before the bomb or after the bomb?

Ada   After the bomb.

Librarian   So, you mean the occupation of Japan by the US Army . . .

Ada   Yes.

Librarian   Follow me, please. (*They cross to another shelf.*) This section is about occupation of Japan by US Army. What was the name again?

Ada   Michael Osborne.

Librarian (*he looks on a shelf*)   M, N, O, P. Oh! I'm sorry, it doesn't exist.

Ada   What do you mean, it doesn't exist?

Librarian   If we don't have it, it doesn't exist.

Ada   Listen, I know it exists. It's a book with articles and photos taken right after the war.

Librarian   Ah! ah! ah! Photography. That would be in the World War II iconography section. Follow me please. (*They cross again.*)

Ada   But wouldn't it be with photography rather than iconography?

Librarian   Never mind ma'am, in the army, photography and iconography are the same. So you said . . . Michael . . .

Ada   . . . Osborne.

Librarian (*he looks on a shelf*)   M. N. O. Oh! *Images of Post-War Japan, 1945 through 1946*, edited by Michael Osborne.

Ada   Thank you very much. I have to trouble you with one last question. Do I have to be a member of the library in order to borrow this book?

Librarian   Sorry, it's for consultation only. After you're done, put it back on the shelf or leave it on the table near the exit.

Ada   So, I assume that photocopies are also out of the question?

Librarian   Is the Pope Catholic?

He exits stage left. **Ada** *flips through the book, stops at a page and looks at it with great interest. Two of the panels slide open and a* **Doctor** *in a lab coat enters and goes to* **Ada**. *The* **Doctor** *puts her stethoscope on* **Ada**'s *chest and the sound of a rapid heartbeat is heard.*

Doctor   Is there any history of heart disease in your family?

Ada   No.

Doctor   Have you personally ever had any heart trouble?

Ada   No.

Doctor   Then why is your heart beating so fast?

Ada   I'm going to see Jeffrey.

Doctor   Who is Jeffrey?

Ada   Someone I once was in love with.

Doctor   Do you still love him?

Ada   Yes, of course.

Doctor   Does he love you?

Ada   I don't know . . . and I'm not sure if it matters any longer . . . he's dying, you see . . .

She looks around her, puts the book in her shoulder bag, and exits stage right. The **Doctor** *leaves through the center panels, which slide open for her.*

3: Café terrasse

Through the open center panels, several actors enter carrying tables and chairs; they place two tables on the porch and three in the rock garden, creating the scene of a café. Recorded soft jazz plays. At the downstage right table, a middle-aged couple sit together speaking Quebecois French. At the center downstage table, a young man sits alone facing upstage. A young couple speaking French sit at the downstage left table. At the upstage left table, an attractive young woman in a trenchcoat, sunglasses, and a headscarf sits, facing downstage.

(NOTE: All the dialogues in this scene – with the exception of **Ada***'s and* **Jeffrey***'s – are improvised at each performance by the actors.)*

Ada *enters through the center doors and greets the waiter, who shows her to the upstage right table. She orders tea from him.*

The **Doctor** *enters through the open center doors and goes to the French couple's table. Through the* **Doctor***'s stethoscope, we hear the amplified conversation at each table she approaches. The French woman is telling a long story of sexual dysfunction and intrigue. The* **Doctor** *goes to the Quebecois couple's table. They are bickering about the pronunciation of Dutch painters' names over an open guidebook. The* **Doctor** *goes to the young woman's table and amplifies the dialogue between the waiter and the woman. She orders in Italian and flirts with the waiter.*

Meanwhile, **Jeffrey 1** *enters. His hair is gray and slicked back; he wears glasses. He and* **Ada** *embrace and sit down. The* **Doctor** *crosses to* **Ada** *and* **Jeffrey***, and amplifies their conversation.*

Ada   What hotel are you staying at?

Jeffrey   The Damrak.

Ada   Isn't that in the middle of the red-light district? . . . You really could come to my place, you know . . . Really, it's all right . . .

Jeffrey   Thanks Ada, I know, but I'm sort of jet-lagged, so I'd rather be on my own.

Ada   All right, but let me know if you change your mind . . . So have you spoken to your brother lately?

The waiter re-enters and goes to the French couple's table, then to the Italian woman's.

Jeffrey   Actually, I saw him a few months ago. He came to New York for the jazz festival with his quartet . . . but of course I've spoken to him since and he told me you were cutting a record?

Ada   Yes, I am . . . Songs by Poulenc. I really love them. In fact, I have a session this afternoon. You can come if you like. Things are going well just now.

. . .

Jeffrey   Speaking of recordings, I brought you one from New York. It's a new release of klezmer music . . .

Ada   The new Feidman! Thank you, we can't get it here yet. And how are you?

Jeffrey   I'm fine.

*The **Doctor** goes to the Quebecois' table, where they are talking about food. Then she goes to the French couple's table, where the woman continues to tell her explicit story. She then crosses back to **Ada** and **Jeffrey**.*

Ada   I would like you to give this book to your brother next time you see him. Did Jeffrey ever tell you that he doesn't have a photo of his mother . . . The way he knew her as a child? The only existing photo was the one your father took. And that very one his grandmother destroyed right after his mother died. I found this book and in it are photos taken by your father. And look, here's a photo of Nozomi.

Jeffrey   Oh my God . . . Jeffrey is going to be so happy to get this. You know, I've realized only recently that my father was also confronted with death at a very early age . . . And now, because of my condition, I'm starting to understand his fascination with pain and suffering . . . death and decay . . .

*The waiter brings **Jeffrey** a glass of wine. As the waiter exits, so do the **Doctor** and the Quebecoise; we hear her asking the waiter for the phone. The **Doctor** re-enters and goes to **Jeffrey** and **Ada**.*

Ada   Tell me more about this conference you came to Amsterdam for.

Jeffrey   It's not a conference, Ada. It's a program for people with terminal diseases.

Ada   Jeffrey, I'm sorry . . . I completely misunderstood . . . what is it exactly . . . a psychological aid program?

Jeffrey   No Ada . . . as I said, it's for people with terminal diseases who have looked at all their options and who have come to the conclusion that it is better for them to end it now.

Ada   I don't understand . . .

Jeffrey   I am talking about assisted suicide, Ada. You see, the doctors have told me that the reason I had that last bout with pneumonia was because they don't have any medication that has any effect on my immune system any longer.

Ada   But Jeffrey, for God's sake, you're rushing things . . . They are developing new drugs every day . . . look at yourself, you're healthy!

Jeffrey   Ada, I just can't lie to myself anymore . . . I have AIDS, I'm going to die. I've seen my father go through the final stages of his illness. I've seen Mickey and many others go. I have made a choice. I don't want to become a vegetable. I've decided that I want to die with a certain amount of dignity.

The waiter and the **Doctor** *go to the Italian woman's table; the single man has moved up to sit with her, and they are flirting. The* **Doctor** *goes back to* **Ada** *and* **Jeffrey**.

Jeffrey   What's more, Ada . . . I'm gonna need your help. You see, in order to be eligible for this program, one has to be a Dutch citizen. To become one, either I live and work here for five years, which obviously is out of the question . . . or I marry a Dutch citizen . . .

Ada *stands up, very upset. She pushes her chair over violently and tries to leave.* **Jeffrey** *stops her.*

Ada   You know how much I've always loved you. Now you're asking me to marry you to help you commit suicide! I hate you!

She runs out of the café. **Jeffrey** *grabs his shoulder bag and follows her.*

4: Red Light 2

The other café patrons clear away the tables and chairs that are on the porch and exit, except for a man, who stands on the stage left side of the porch with his back to the audience. The light switches to black light

and the prostitutes re-enter. **Ada** *runs across the stage;* **Jeffrey**
*follows a few moments later, calling her name, then gives up and turns
back and crosses slowly back the way he came. The prostitutes knock on
the door frames and stamp their heels to catch his attention. He doesn't
notice and exits stage right.*

5: Recording studio

*The prostitutes exit. The lights change so we can see that the back wall
is covered with soundproofing material; the scene has shifted to a
recording studio.* **Ada** *enters and places a sheet of music on a music
stand. She sings 'Banalités/Sanglots', a song by Apollinaire with
music by Poulenc, about dreamers who tear our their hearts because of
love. She sings in French, which is translated using supertitles.
Halfway through the song, young* **Jeffrey 1** *enters, looking just as he
did in 'Two Jeffreys'. As he enters, the sound of* **Ada***'s singing recedes
and the lights dim, indicating that he is appearing to* **Ada** *in her
imagination.* **Jeffrey** *crosses to* **Ada** *and puts his hands up as if
pressing against a window. She reaches out and touches his face. He
exits. The lights come up again and she finishes her song, then exits.*

6: Exit

*In dim light, the back wall of the recording studio slowly flips up to
become the slanted ceiling of* **Ada***'s apartment. There is a window
upstage, at which* **Jeffrey 1** *stands, looking out. Slowly, a sofa and
table slide onstage, and a door slides into place stage left. The lights
come up.* **Jeffrey 2** *enters, his hair also gray, carrying a tray with a
bottle of champagne and glasses on it. He puts the tray down on a small
table stage right, on which sits the Japanese wedding doll from
'Moving Pictures'.*

Jeffrey 1 *and* **Jeffrey 2** *embrace.*

Jeffrey 1   It's so good to see you again . . . Let's have a
glass of champagne.

Jeffrey 2 *pours champagne;* **Ada** *and* **Hanako**, *a petite Japanese woman with black hair and dark glasses, enter stage left;* **Ada** *is guiding* **Hanako**, *who is blind.*

Jeffrey 1   Hanako, would you like a glass of champagne?

Hanako   Yes, please.

Jeffrey 1 (*offering champagne*)   Ada? I would like to propose a toast . . . to all of you who I love so very much. Cheers.

Jeffrey 2 *and* **Hanako**   Kampai!

Ada   L'chaim!

They all toast. **Ada** *puts on a tape of klezmer music. All sit on the sofa but* **Jeffrey 1**, *who picks up the book* **Ada** *found in the library scene off the table and hands it to* **Jeffrey 2**.

Jeffrey 1   Jeffrey, this book here is from Ada. It contains some pictures taken by Dad. There's a photo of your mother . . . look here.

Jeffrey 2 (*examines the book with awe*)   That's incredible . . . Where did you get this?

Ada   There is a war library here in Amsterdam; they have everything, so . . .

Jeffrey 2   Thank you very much. It's fantastic!

Jeffrey 1   Hanako? How is little David?

Hanako   He's fine. He's really fine. He's just fourteen now . . . He's going to the lycée.

Jeffrey 1 (*going to pick up his camera*)   I want to take a picture of the three of you.

He takes a picture of the other three; then **Ada** *takes a picture of the two* **Jeffreys** *and* **Hanako**. **Susan**, *the* **Doctor** – *dressed now in street clothes and carrying a doctor's bag* – *enters stage left and knocks on the front door.* **Ada** *lets her in, kisses her hello, as does* **Jeffrey 1**.

Jeffrey 1   Susan, this is my brother Jeffrey . . . And his wife Hanako.

Hanako   Nice to meet you.

Susan   Nice to meet you.

They all shake hands and sit down. The following conversation is stilted and uncomfortable.

Jeffrey 1   Would you like a glass of champagne?

Susan   Yes, a small glass, please . . .

Jeffrey 1   My brother Jeffrey is a jazz musician.

Susan   I love jazz . . . And what do you do, Hanako?

Hanako   I'm a translator.

Susan   From English to Japanese?

Hanako   No. From French to Japanese.

Susan   Do you live here in Amsterdam?

Jeffrey 2   No, we live in Paris, but we're going back to Japan in a few months. To Hiroshima, in my mother's house . . . Do you live here in Amsterdam?

Susan   Yes . . . I specialize in infectious diseases . . .

A long silence. **Susan**, *at a nod from* **Jeffrey 1** *stands up and starts to unpack her doctor's bag. She crosses behind the door, and comes back with an IV stand which she sets up next to the sofa. She hangs two full IV bags on the stand and prepares vials of medicine and syringes.* **Ada**, *getting increasingly agitated, goes off stage.*

Jeffrey 2   Is she all right?

Jeffrey 1   No.

Ada *returns, and sits down.* **Susan** *puts an IV needle into* **Jeffrey 1**'s *arm.* **Ada** *gets up again, goes off stage and comes back carrying her trenchcoat. She leans over* **Jeffrey 1** *who is sitting on the sofa. Their dialogue is barely audible.*

Ada   Jeffrey, I can't stay.

Jeffrey 1   It's all right, Ada.

Ada   . . . love you.

She kisses him, and leaves through the front door, crying. **Jeffrey 2** *follows her.*

Jeffrey 2   Ada . . . ?

Ada   I'll be all right . . . (*Crying, she exits stage left.*)

Jeffrey 2 *comes back inside, closes the door, and sits next to his brother.*

Jeffrey 2   We'll take good care of her.

Hanako *slips down onto the floor, puts her arms around* **Jeffrey 1***'s legs and rests her head on his knees.* **Susan** *injects a liquid into a tube under one of the IV bags. She nods to* **Jeffrey 1**. *After a long silence, he reaches over, and twists the tubes underneath the IV bags, opening up the flow of IV liquid. He puts his head on* **Jeffrey 2***'s shoulder. Blackout.*

Short pause in the dark.

Lights up. Hours have passed. **Jeffrey 2** *is smoking outside the open door.* **Hanako** *is sleeping in the chair.* **Ada** *is standing over* **Jeffrey 1***'s body, which is lying on the sofa.* **Susan** *takes the IV tube out of* **Jeffrey 1***'s arm and places that arm over the other one.* **Ada** *covers* **Jeffrey 1***'s body with a duvet, takes off his glasses, wakes* **Hanako** *up, and goes out front to get* **Jeffrey 2**. **Jeffrey 2** *comes inside and looks at his brother's body.* **Ada** *closes the door. Blackout.*

4: THE MIRROR
Hiroshima, 1986; Terezin, 1943

1: Prologue

Ada *is heard in voice-over.*

Ada Hiroshima, January 1st, 1986. Dear Ms Čapek, You
will be surprised to hear from me here in Japan. I read in the
English newspaper that your exhibition in Tokyo will be
opening in a few days. There has been a death in our family
and I have come here with my friends to recuperate and to
spend some time with them before I return to my
engagements in Europe. So, here we are, both in Japan . . .
and I am hoping, after all these years of corresponding, to
finally meet you in person. I will be glad to come to see you in
Tokyo but I wondered if you wouldn't be interested in seeing
Hiroshima? You have an open invitation from my brother-
in-law Jeffrey Yamashita and his wife Hanako to come visit
us. Let me know what you think of this idea. I'll adjust to
whatever your time schedule may be and will, if necessary,
get onto the next northbound train in order to see you. I am
waiting to hear from you with anticipation and with much
affection. Ada Weber.

2: Jana's arrival

*Lights up. The porch is covered in tatami mats and the doors are shut.
We are inside the house. The sound of thunder is heard.* **Jana**, *wearing
an elegant black silk pantsuit, and* **Ada**, *in a kimono, enter.*

Ada So, this is the room you'll be staying in, Ms Čapek.

Jana Jana.

Ada I'm sorry . . . Jana. Here is a wardrobe if you want to
hang up some clothes, and at the center of the closet is a shelf
with blankets. It does get chilly at night sometimes, so here in

the middle part are some extra blankets . . . I've shown you the bathroom . . . Oh yes, I hope you like fish?

Jana   I do.

Ada   The reason I'm asking is that Jeffrey and Hanako always make Japanese breakfast, so if you want to have something more western-style . . . eggs and toast, you should let me know.

Jana   No, no, it's OK. I do love fish, even in the morning.

Ada   You're tougher than I am! I only drink tea. Well, I'll let you sleep. Thank you for coming all the way from Tokyo to see me.

Jana   I'm really looking forward to seeing Hiroshima tomorrow.

Ada   After I wrote to you I imagined you here . . . and I realized that in a way you ought to feel at home in Hiroshima. After all, it is a city of survivors . . . (*Pause.*) Will you be all right? Is there anything else I could get you?

Jana   No. Thank you. I'll be all right.

Ada   Good night, then.

Jana   Good night.

Ada *exits.* **Jana** *takes off her shirt, hangs it up, and puts on a silk robe. She opens the center doors and does a slight take when she sees there are mirrors behind them. She opens the three center doors and sits down in front of the mirrors. Looking at herself, she lies on her side with her back to the audience. The tinkle of chimes is heard, and the lights fade downstage and come up upstage. The mirrors turn transparent so we can see behind them. A young girl with red hair in a pink dress is lying behind the mirrors in an identical position to* **Jana**; *a yellow star is sewn on her dress. It is* **Jana** *when she was a girl. All the action involving* **young Jana** *in this section takes place behind this wall of mirrors. Throughout the section, whenever the action switches to* **older Jana**, *the sound of thunder can be heard.*

3: Terezin – Deportation 1

Pulsing string music plays, with an increasingly urgent beat. A line of men and women in winter coats and hats, with yellow stars sewn to their lapels, cross the stage. All carry musical instrument cases and suitcases. The wall behind the now-transparent mirrors is also covered with mirrors, so that the images of the people walking are repeated multiple times behind them. As the music speeds up, they walk faster and faster and break into a run. A man stops and shakes **young Jana** *awake; she gets up, hesitates and decides to follow the crowd. Blackout upstage;* **older Jana** *stirs and turns over.*

4: The Dormitory

Lights up upstage. The space between the two sets of mirrors is filled with wooden bunk beds; the women we saw in the previous scene are milling around and lying on the beds. **Young Jana** *enters and climbs up onto a bed; one of the women,* **Rachel Goldberg**, *approaches and speaks to her. The dialogue is in German, translated with supertitles.*

Goldberg   Was machst du da? Das ist mein Bett. Hörst du? Verstehst du kein Deutsch? Das ist mein Bett. Wie alt bist du eigentlich? Du solltest im Kinderheim sein. [What are you doing here? This is my bed. Listen. Don't you understand German? This is my bed. How old are you anyway? You should be in the children's home.]

Terrified, **young Jana** *pretends she doesn't understand.* **Sarah Weber** *(played by the same actress who played* **Ada***) is sitting on one of the beds reading. She interrupts* **Goldberg**.

Sarah   So, das reicht. Die Kleine kann bei mir schlafen. Komm, komm zu mir. Bring deine Sachen mit. (. . .) Also sprichst du wirklich kein Deutsch? Du, ich kann kein tschechisch. (. . .) Mluvite nemĕcky? [Enough. The girl can sleep in my bed. Come, come to me. Bring your things with you. (**Jana** *moves her things down to* **Sarah***'s bed and stands next to her silently.*) I really speak very little Czech. (*In Czech.*) So do you speak German?]

Jana   (. . .) Ja. Ein bisschen. [(*In German.*) Yes, a little.]

Sarah   Gut. Also . . . wei heisst du? [Good . . .what is your name?]

Jana   Jana Čapekova. Und du? [Jana Čapek. And yours?]

Sarah   Sarah Weber . . . Weberova. Bist du ganz alleine hier? [Sarah Weber. Are you here all alone?]

Jana   (. . .) Was ist das? [(*She doesn't answer. Looking at* **Sarah**'s *book.*) What is that?]

Sarah   Das? Das ist eine Oper. Weisst du ich bin eine Sängerin. [It's an opera score. I am a singer.]

Jana   Du hast so schöne Haare. [You have such beautiful hair.]

Sarah   Willst du sie bürsten? [Do you want to brush it?]

Jana   Ja. [Yes.] (*She brushes* **Sarah**'s *hair.*)

Sarah   Wie alt bist du? [How old are you?]

Jana   (. . .) Jedenáct . . . [(*She gestures eleven with her hands and speaks in Czech.*) Eleven.]

Sarah   (. . .) Elf. [(*In German.*) Eleven.]

Jana   Elf. Und du. Wie alt bist du? [Eleven. And you? How old are you?]

Sarah   Ja, ich bin sehr alt . . . (. . .) dreimal so alt wie du. [Oh, I'm very old . . . (*She indicates her age with her hands.*) Three times as old as you.]

Jana   Ja, das ist sehr alt! [Yes, that's very old!]

Sarah   (. . .) Komm mal her. (. . .) Schau, schau wie schön du bist . . . was heisst schön auf tschechisch? [(*She puts lipstick on, then gestures to* **Jana**.) Come here . . . (*She puts lipstick on* **Jana**, *then shows* **Jana** *her image in a silver hand mirror.*) Look how beautiful you are. What is the word for beautiful in Czech?]

The lights come down upstage and up downstage; **older Jana** *sits up and answers* **Sarah**'s *question.*

Older Jana   Krásný!

She opens one of the door panels, revealing another mirror. She sits down, leaning with her back on one of the still-closed doors.

5: The magician

Lights up upstage. The women are sleeping in the barracks. **Sarah** *and* **young Jana** *are sharing a bed.* **Maurice,** *a man in black trousers and a black vest with a red triangle on his lapel, is standing in the barracks unfolding a wooden measuring stick. He goes to measure* **Jana** *and she wakes up and jumps out of bed.* **Maurice** *shushes her.*

Jana   Was machst du hier im Frauenheim? [What are you doing in the women's barracks?]

Maurice   Ich messe dich. [I'm measuring you.]

Jana   Warum? [Why?]

Maurice   Um zu sehen ob du in die Kiste passt . . . [To see if you'll fit in the box . . .]

Jana   Was für eine Kiste? [Which box?]

Maurice   Meine Zauberkiste. Ich bin ein Zauberer. (. . .) Maurice Zimmermann aus Paris, France. Hör mal! Ich habe morgen Abend eine Vorstellung und ich brauche eine Assistentin in genau deiner Grösse. Willst du meine Assistentin sein? [My magic box. I'm a magician . . . (*Shakes her hand.*) I'm Maurice Zimmermann, from Paris, France. Listen! I'm doing a number for tomorrow's show and I need an assistant just your size. Would you like to be my assistant?]

Jana   Was muss ich tun? [What do I have to do?]

Maurice   Es ist ganz einfach. Du gehst auf die Bühne, und ich lasse dich verschwinden! [It's very simple. You just go on stage, and I'll make you disappear!]

Jana   Aber holst du mich auch wieder zurück? [But will you make me reappear?]

Maurice   Natürlich . . . es ist ein Trick. Du steigst in eine Kiste und versteckst dich hinter einem Spiegel . . . Dann kann das Publikum dich nicht sehen. [Of course . . . It's a trick. You get into a box and hide behind a mirror . . . So the audience cannot see you are still there.]

Jana   Sind alle Leute die verschwunden sind hinter Spiegeln versteckt? [Are all people who have disappeared hiding behind mirrors?]

Lights down upstage and up downstage. **Older Jana** *opens two more of the doors to reveal more mirrors, and sits down facing the mirrors.*

6: Dressing room 1

Lights up upstage. **Young Jana** *runs on calling* **Sarah**'s *name and pushes open the two center upstage mirrors. They swing open to reveal* **Sarah** *in a dressing room; she is sitting at a vanity table with a mirror that faces the audience.*

Jana   Sarah! Ich helfe dem Zauberer heute Abend und er hat gesagt dass ich ein Kostüm brauche! [Sarah! I'm supposed to help the magician tonight and he said I need a costume!]

Sarah   Das ist ja ganz toll. Komm wie suchen dir etwas. Nimm die Sachen dort . . . [Wonderful! Come. Let's look for something . . . Take those things . . .]

Jana *and* **Sarah** *pick up some costumes that are lying on the floor in* **Sarah**'s *dressing room, bring them further downstage, and kneel down to look through them.* **Jana** *picks up a yellow kimono.*

Jana   Ah das . . . das ist wunderbar! [Oh, this . . . this is beautiful!]

Sarah   Ja, aber das ist für mich. (. . .) Schau das ist genau was du brauchst. Das passt dir perfekt. [Yes, but that is for me. (*She picks up a little black cape and puts it on* **Jana**.) Look, this is just what you need. This fits you perfectly.]

Jana   Ich sehe wie ein Künstler aus! [I look like an artist!]

Sarah   Jawohl. (. . .) Miluje tě. [Yes. (*They stand up;* **Sarah** *grabs* **Jana** *and waltzes with her, humming 'The Blue Danube', then picks* **Jana** *up and spins her around; they laugh together.* **Sarah** *puts* **Jana** *down and kisses her. She speaks in Czech.*) I love you.]

Sarah *picks up a basket of make-up and they sit down again with the costumes.* **Sarah** *starts putting up her hair.*

Jana   (. . .) Für was ist das Kostüm? [(*Referring to the kimono.*) What is that costume for?]

Sarah   Das ist für Butterfly. Es ist ein japanisches Kostüm und heisst kimono. Schau. Schön nicht wahr. Sag was musst du eigentlich mit dem Zauberer machen? [It is for Butterfly. It's a Japanese costume called a kimono. Look. Isn't it beautiful! What do you have to do in the magician's show?]

Jana   Was ist Butterfly? [What is Butterfly?]

Sarah   Butterfly ist eine japanische Frau die einen ausländischen Mann heiratet. [Butterfly is a Japanese woman who marries a foreign man.]

Jana   Und was macht der Mann? [And what does this man do?]

Sarah   Er geht weit, weit weg, nach Amerika und sie wartet sehr sehr lange auf ihn. [He goes back to America and she waits for him a very, very long time.]

Jana   Ja . . . und dann? [Yes . . . and then?]

Sarah   (. . .) Siehst du so tragen di Japanerinnen ihr Haar . . . mit Stäbchen . . . sie essen auch damit das hast du bestimmt nicht gewusst oder? [(*She puts sticks in her hair.*) Look. This is how Japanese women wear their hair . . . with sticks in it . . . They even eat with sticks. Did you know that?]

Jana   Nein . . . aber was passiert dann mit der Frau? [No . . . but what happens to the woman?]

Sarah   Der Mann kommt zurück und weil die Frau eine andere Rasse ist als er nimmt er ihr das Kind weg. Es ist furchtbar. [The man returns, and because the woman is of a different race, he takes their child away with him. It's terrible.]

Jana   Und was tut die Frau dann? [And what does the woman do then?]

Sarah Die Frau ist natürlich sehr traurig ohne ihr Kind
. . . so traurig dass sie sich tötet. Komm, schmink mich!
[Without her child, she is very sad, of course . . . so sad that
she kills herself. Come do my make-up.]

Jana Ist das Kind jüdisch? (. . .) Warum weinst du? (. . .)
Hast du auch ein Kind? (. . .) Wie heisst dein Kind? [Is the
child Jewish? (**Sarah** *gets up, walks downstage, away from* **Jana**,
and starts to cry.) Why are you crying? . . . (**Jana** *comes to
comfort her.*) Do you also have a child? (**Sarah** *nods.*) What's
the child's name?]

Sarah Ada.

Jana Ada.

Sarah *walks upstage into her dressing room, still crying.* **Jana**,
*turning, sees in the mirror that her dress is stained. She lifts it. There is
blood on her underwear. She starts to whimper and turns to* **Sarah**.
Sarah *puts her arm around her and takes her into the dressing room,
shutting the mirror panels behind her.*

7: The magic trick 1

Sprightly recorded music plays. **Maurice** *enters, wearing a top hat
and jacket over his previous costume and carrying a big black box. He
polishes a mirror with a red, white, and blue handkerchief, then inserts
the mirror into the box to give the illusion that the box is a table.*

*The dressing-room doors swing open to reveal the inhabitants of the
camp gathered on the barrack bunk beds, facing* **Maurice** *and the
audience. They applaud.* **Maurice** *starts his magic show; he
performs with his back to the audience. He speaks in German,
translated with supertitles.*

Maurice Guten Abend meine Damen und Herren!
Herzlich Willkommen! Ich freue mich die Ehre zu haben
diese Vorstellung heute Abend beginnen zu dürfen. Ich hoffe
das meine Zauberei Ihnen gefällt. Aber zuerst darf ich Ihnen
meine junge Assistentin vorstellen. Jana Čapek! (. . .) Guten
Abend Jana. [Good evening, ladies and gentlemen.
Welcome! I am happy to have the honor to open this

evening's performance. I hope that my magic show will
please you. But first, let me introduce my young assistant to
you. Jana Čapek! (*The crowd applauds.* **Jana** *dashes on wearing
her cape and a bow in her hair.*) Good evening, Jana!]

Jana   Guten Abend! [Good evening!]

Maurice   Wie alt bist du Jana? [How old are you, Jana?]

Jana   Ich bin elf. [I am eleven.]

Maurice   Elf! Bitte, Jana, hol' jetzt die kiste! [Eleven!
Jana, please go and get the box.]

Jana *goes out and comes back, carrying a large cardboard box
decorated with paintings of stars and moons and places it on top of the
black box.*

Maurice   Meine Damen und Herren ich werde dieses
kleine Mädchen vor Ihren Augen heute Abend
verschwinden lassen! [Ladies and gentlemen, before your
very eyes I will make this young girl disappear!]

Jana *pretends to panic and to run away.* **Maurice** *catches her.*

Maurice   Hab' keine Angst, Jana. Steig' jetzt in die Kiste.
[Don't be afraid, Jana. Now get into the box.]

*He helps her climb onto the black box, then to step into the decorated
carton.*

Jana   Hoffentlich erscheine ich wieder! Lebt wohl!
[Hopefully I will reappear! Farewell!]

She sits down into the carton as **Maurice** *closes the flaps on top of her.*

Maurice   Gut . . . ich mache den Deckel zu. Meine
Damen und Herren . . . kein Trick! (. . .) Jana bist du da?
[Good . . . now I will close the lid. Ladies and gentlemen, no
trick! . . . (*He knocks on the side of the box.*) Jana, are you there?]

Jana   Ja, ich bin hier! [Yes, I am here!]

Maurice   Meine Damen und Herren jetzt werde ich Jana
in die Welt des Unsichtbaren schicken. Hokus pokus fidibus
dreimal schwarzer Kater! [Now I will transport Jana into the
realm of the invisible. Hocus pocus, three times black cat!]

Jana *slips out of the carton through a back panel and hides in the black box.* **Maurice** *picks up the carton and holds it up so that the barracks audience can see it's empty.*

Maurice   Sehen Sie! Zauberei! (. . .) Wo könnte sie sein. Sie war doch gerade hier? Ist sie mit dem Zug verreist? Aber nein . . . sie ist doch nur ein kleines Mädchen (. . .) Jetzt meine Damen und Herren werde ich Jana vor Ihren Auge wieder zum erscheinen bringen . . . Eins, zwei, drei Hokus pokus fidibus dreimal schwarzer Kater. (. . .) Jana bist du da? [See! Magic! (*The barracks audience applauds.*) Where could she be? She was just there! Is she taking a train trip? But no . . . she is only a little girl! (*During his patter,* **Jana** *climbs up from the box back into the carton.*) Now, before your very eyes, ladies and gentlemen, I will make Jana reappear! One, two, three, hocus pocus, three times black cat! (*Knocks on the carton.*) Jana, are you there?]

Jana   Ja, ich bin hier! [Yes, I am here!]

Jana *pops out of the top of the carton. The barracks audience applauds. She jumps off the top of the box, holding the carton around her waist, and scampers off the stage.* **Maurice** *chases after her in pretend rage as the barracks audience laughs. They return and take a bow.*

The light on them fades out and the lights downstage come up. **Older Jana** *paces around the room during the following recorded announcement.*

Loudspeaker   Achtung, Achtung eine Durchsage: Hier spricht der Judenälteste mit dem Tagesbefehl der SS-Kommandatur für morgen den 23 Juni. Die Delegation des Roten Kreuzes trifft um 14:00Uhr in Theresienstadt ein. Die Teilnehmer der verschiedenen Veranstaltungen haben zu den, an den Anschlagetafeln angegeben Zeiten, pünktlich zu erscheinen. SS-Obersturmführer Rahm wird die Delegation begleiten. Alle an den Vorführungen Beteiligten haben sich ständig bereitzuhalten. Alle privaten Kabaretts und Kameradschaftsabende jeglicher Art, sind am morgigen Tage strengstens untersagt. Zuwiderhandelnden wird mit schwersten Strafen gedroht. End der Durchsage. [Attention, attention: an announcement. This is the Jewish Elder

announcing the daily command from the SS-camp
headquarters for tomorrow, June 23rd. The delegation from
the Red Cross will arrive in Theresienstadt at 14:00 hours.
The participants of the various performances are to appear
punctually at the times listed on the bulletin boards. SS-
Obersturmführer Rahm will be accompanying the
delegation. All performers and participants are to be in
readiness at all times. Tomorrow all private cabarets and
performances of any kind are strictly prohibited. Those
acting in defiance of this command are threatened with
severest punishment. End of announcement.]

8: Deportation call

*Lights dim downstage, come up upstage on a painting studio in the
camp.* **Sarah** *sits upstage, wearing her kimono over her gray suit,
posing. Tinkling music-box music plays. Three prisoners are
'painting' her; their canvases are represented by mirrors and they mime
brushes. A woman wearing a Red Cross armband enters, followed by a
soldier. She examines each of the paintings and says a few words to the
prisoners. She exits. The* **Soldier** *takes out slips of paper and starts to
read, in German. His words are not translated into supertitles. As each
prisoner's name is called he or she walks forward and takes the paper.*

Soldier   Rachel Goldberg, transport 35-G. Jana Čapek.
Jana Čapek. (**Jana** *is not there.*) Benjamin Wiesenthal,
transport 35-H. Moishe Podicz, transport 35-G. Maurice
Zimmermann. (**Maurice** *is not there.*) Sarah Weber,
transport 35-G.

Sarah *tears up her piece of paper and exits. The prisoners pick up their
easels and exit.*

9: The magic trick 2

Maurice *and* **Jana** *enter; he carries a suitcase. They pack together.
The sound of Puccini's* Madame Butterfly *is heard. They speak in
German and French. The German portions of their conversation are
translated using supertitles; the French portions are not translated.*

Jana   Sie singen auf Italienisch aber ich verstehe es! Sarah
hat mir die Geschichte erzählt. Jetzt singt Herr Pinkerton.
Er hat sich ein Haus und eine Frau gekauft. Die Frau ist
Japanerin und er will in ihr Land gehen das Nagasaki Japan
heisst. Sie haben ein Kind zusammen. Die Frau heisst
Butterfly und sie trägt einen kimono. Weisst du was
'Butterfly' bedeutet . . . Schmetterling! (. . .) Maurice . . .
wo bist du? [They are singing in Italian, but I can
understand them. Sarah told me the story. Here, Mr
Pinkerton is going to sing. He bought a house and a wife. The
wife is Japanese and he wants to go to her country. Her
country is called Nagasaki, Japan. They have a baby
together. The woman's name is Butterfly. Do you know what
Butterfly means? (**Maurice** *has sat down on a small box and is
staring into space.* **Jana** *is disappointed that he is not paying attention
to her.*) Maurice, where are you?]

Maurice   Ich war in Paris. (. . .) 'Paris, c'est une
ronde . . .' Garçon, un café! [I was in Paris. (*Sings.*) 'Paris,
c'est une ronde.' (*In French.*) Waiter, a coffee!]

Jana   (*tries to imitate him*)   Garzon, un café!

Maurice   (. . .) Nein, nicht 'garzon' . . . 'garçon'! (. . .)
Ma pauvre enfant, avec un accent pareil, vaut mieux se jeter
au fond de la Seine ou du haut de la tour Eiffel. Mais pour
cela, il faudrait sortir d'ici. Et pour sortir d'ici, il faudrait un
miracle ou un tour de magie incroyable. [(*Correcting her
pronunciation, in German.*) No, not 'garzon' . . . 'garçon'! (*In
French.*) My poor child, with an accent like that, it would be
better to throw yourself into the Seine or off the top of the
Eiffel Tower. But to do that, you'd have to get out of here.
And that would take an incredible magic trick.]

Jana *makes him stand up and puts the box on his head. She folds the
measuring stick into a wand and waves it around his head.*

Jana   Hokus pokus fidibus dreimal schwarzer Kater!
Maurice bist du da? (. . .) Maurice bist du in Paris? [(*In
German.*) Hocus pocus, three times black cat! Maurice, are
you there? (*Pause.*) Maurice, are you in Paris?]

Maurice   Nein, merde . . . ich bin hier! [(*In German.*) No,
shit . . . I am here!]

Blackout.

10: Deportation 2

*The music from the deportation scene (scene 3) plays and the procession
from scene 3 is repeated, in reverse. In front of the mirrors, **older
Jana** paces back and forth, countering the movement of the prisoners.
Behind the mirrors, **young Jana**, lost in the crowd, desperately looks
for **Sarah**, calling her name. She runs back to the dressing room.*

11: Dressing room 2

Jana *opens the mirrors to* **Sarah**'s *dressing room, and discovers*
Sarah's *body. She has hanged herself. Only the lower half of her body
is visible.* **Jana** *cries out; at the same moment* **older Jana** *freezes in
her tracks downstage.* **Young Jana** *grabs a chair, which has been
knocked over, stands on it and throws her arms around* **Sarah**'s *body,
crying. She steps down, picks up* **Sarah**'s *silver hand mirror from the
table and looks in it, as the mirror doors close in front of her.*

12: The escape

*A soldier enters, then a prisoner carrying his suitcase, who hands his
deportation order to the soldier. At a signal from the soldier the prisoner
puts down his case and one of the mirrors swings open, suggesting the
door of a train. The prisoner walks through the train door. Another
prisoner enters, gives his deportation order to the soldier, and goes onto
the train. The process is repeated several times.* **Maurice** *and* **Jana**
enter with **Maurice**'s *magic box.* **Jana** *gives her order to the soldier
and puts down her case, but, while the soldier is busy with another
prisoner,* **Maurice** *pushes her inside the magic box and enters the
train. The mirror doors close.*

The first measures of the finale of Madame Butterfly *play. The
soldier carries off all the cases, then rolls the box offstage with* **Jana** *in*

it. A soprano's voice is heard singing the finale of Madame
Butterfly.

13: Finale

Older Jana *kneels before the mirrors. The upstage mirror doors
swing open.* **Sarah** *enters, wearing the wedding kimono from
'Moving Pictures' over her suit. It is she who is singing. As she sings,
she slowly moves forward towards the upstage mirrors – and* **older
Jana** *– touching the mirror as if to reach through to* **Jana** *on the other
side.*

Sarah   'O a me sceso dal trono dell'alto Paradiso, guarda
ben fiso, fiso di tua madre la facia che te'n resti una tracia,
guarda ben! Amore, addio! Addio piccolo amor! Va. Gioca
. . . gioca.' [You, you little god, my love. You came to me
from Paradise. Look closely at the face of your mother, so a
trace will remain with you. Look closely! My love, goodbye,
goodbye, little love. Go. Play . . . play.]

*As the music swells, she turns and walks back towards the upstage
mirrors, which are angled so that her image appears in double profile to
the audience. She takes out a dagger and, at the music's climactic point,
stabs herself.*

*Blackout upstage; the lights switch so that the audience can see its own
reflection in the downstage mirrors.*

5: WORDS
Osaka, 1970

1: Le téléphone/The telephone

There is a telephone booth at the stage right corner of the rock garden. The rice-paper doors are in place.

An actor wearing a No theater costume — shōjō mask, elaborate gold kimono and long, bright red wig — enters stage right on the porch. His arms are stretched straight out in front of him and he carries a fan. Music inspired by the No theater plays.

Sophie, *a young woman in minidress and vinyl knee boots, enters stage left in the rock garden, countering the movement of the No character.*

They walk forward at the same slow pace and, at a cue from the music, turn to face the audience. As they turn, **Sophie** *looks down at a small address book she holds. They turn back and continue walking. The No character walks offstage;* **Sophie** *goes into the phone booth. As the door of the booth shuts, the lights go off outside and come on inside the booth. A section of the wooden frame of the house, extreme stage right, swings open at eye level. A* **Translator** *appears and clicks on a light which illuminates his face. The following dialogue is performed with live simultaneous translation by this* **Translator**. **Hanako** *is offstage, not visible.*

Hanako/Translator   Moshi, moshi. [Hello.]

Sophie/Translator   Allo! J'aimerais parler à Madame Hanako Nishikawa, s'il-vous-plaît. [Hello. I would like to talk to Mrs Hanako Nishikawa, please.]

Hanako/Translator   Hanako desu. [This is Hanako.]

Sophie/Translator   Madame Nishikawa? . . . Sophie Maltais à l'appareil. [Mrs Nishikawa? This is Sophie Maltais calling.]

Hanako/Translator   Ah bon, Madame Maltais.
J'attendais votre appel. [Oh, good, Mrs Maltais. I have been
waiting for your call.]

Sophie/Translator   Je suis arrivée hier à Osaka. On m'a
dit que vous vouliez prendre rendez-vous avec moi pour
qu'on regarde ensemble le texte du Feydeau . . . [I arrived in
Osaka yesterday. I received a message that you would like to
meet up with me to look at the Feydeau text.]

Hanako/Translator   Oui, j'ai reçu la traduction
japonaise mais les phrases en japonais sont deux fois plus
longues qu'en français. Alors je me demandais si on pouvait
se rencontrer; vous pourriez lire pour moi quelques extraits,
à la vitesse à laquelle vous allez jouer la pièce . . . Comme ça,
je pourrais faire les coupures et les ajustements . . . [Yes, I
received the Japanese translation, and the Japanese
sentences are twice as long as the French ones. So I was
wondering if we could meet . . . I would really like you to
read me the sentences at the pace you're going to perform
them in the production. So I could make cuts and
adjustments.]

Sophie/Translator   Quand est-ce que vous voulez qu'on
se voie? [When would you like to meet?]

Hanako/Translator   Je suis toujours à Hiroshima, mais
je prends le train demain matin et je serai à Osaka en début
d'après-midi. [I am still in Hiroshima, and I'm going to take
the train tomorrow so I will be in Osaka at the beginning of
the afternoon.]

Sophie/Translator   Trois heures de l'après-midi, ça vous
va? [Is three o'clock good for you?]

Hanako/Translator   Oui, j'ai votre adresse, alors je peux
passer vous voir à l'hôtel? [Yes, I have your address, so shall I
come to your hotel?]

Sophie/Translator   Parfait. [Perfect.]

Hanako/Translator   À demain! [See you tomorrow!]

Sophie/Translator   À demain. Au revoir! [See you tomorrow. Bye.]

Sophie *hangs up, leaves the phone booth, and exits. The* **Translator** *clicks off his light and disappears.*

2: Photomaton 1/Photo booth 1

All set changes in this section are done in view of the audience — there are no blackouts.

A photo booth slides on stage left. A train timetable in Japanese is projected onto the stage right screen; Japanese advertisements appear on the center screen. We are in the Osaka train station. We hear a voice announcing train arrivals and departures in Japanese.

Patricia Hébert *and* **Walter Lapointe** *rush onstage.*
Patricia *has ash-blonde hair and is wearing a mini skirt suit.*
Walter *has long sideburns, is wearing a suit and tie, and carrying a suitcase. They speak in French, and their dialogue is translated using supertitles.*

Patricia   T'as ma valise, là, Walter? [Do you have my suitcase, Walter?]

Walter   Oui, oui, Patricia. [Yes, yes, Patricia.]

Patricia   Bon, y a des taxis par là. [Good, there are some taxis over there.]

Walter   (. . .) Oh, attends un peu Patricia, je viens de me rappeler, j'ai oublié de me faire faire des photos pour mon passeport pour l'expo. Ça sera pas long. [*(Stopping in front of the photo booth.)* Wait, I just remembered. I forgot to get a picture taken for my pass for the expo. It won't be long.]

Patricia   Voyons Walter, tu vas pas faire des photos dans ce machin-truc-là? [Look, Walter, you're not going to have your picture taken in that stupid booth!]

Walter   Ben oui! Pourquoi pas? [Sure! Why not?]

Patricia   Pourquoi tu m'en as pas parlé plus tôt? J'aurais téléphoné à un photographe à Tokyo, il serait passé à l'appartement . . . Tu aurais des photos convenables, au moins, pas la merde que tu vas avoir là-dedans! [Why didn't you mention this before? I could have called a photographer in Tokyo. He could have come to the apartment. You would have gotten decent pictures, not the crap you'll get here.]

Walter   J'en ai besoin aujourd'hui! [I really need them this afternoon!]

Patricia   Bon, d'accord, d'accord, fais tes photos. [Fine, OK, OK, take your pictures.]

Walter   T'aurais pas une pièce de 100 yen sur toi? [Do you have a 100 yen coin on you?]

Patricia   Par dessus le marché, c'est moi qui vais les payer! (. . .) Ah! Walter! . ... Tiens, voilà 100 yen. (. . .) Je pense que j'ai laissé mes Diovol à Tokyo et j'ai mes brûlures d'estomac qui me reprennent, là. (. . .) La bouffe sur ce train, c'était vraiment infect, tu trouves pas? Et puis c'était interminable, ce trajet! Quatre heures, Tokyo–Osaka! Ils appellent ça un 'bullet train'. Moi qui croyais que le Japon était le pays de la technologie! . . . Walter, t'as pris des Diovol avec toi? [And on top of that, I have to pay for them! (*She digs in her purse, finds a coin, and hands it to him.*) Here's 100 yen. (*He goes into the photo booth.*) I think I forgot my Diovol in Tokyo. I have my heartburn again. (*The train schedule stage right is replaced by a live video image of* **Walter** *in the photo booth.*) The food on that train was disgusting, don't you think? And it seemed like the trip would never end. Four hours, Tokyo–Osaka. They call that a bullet train. I thought Japan was the country of technology. Walter, did you bring some Diovol with you?]

Walter   Non. [No.]

There is a flash of light in the booth; **Walter**'s *image freezes for a few seconds as the first picture is being taken; he looks exasperated. Then the live video resumes.*

Patricia   Il va falloir s'arrêter dans une pharmacie parce que moi je peux pas passer la journée comme ça. Déjà que j'ai pas du tout envie de me taper le site de l'expo cet après-midi.

(. . .) . . . Je suppose que ça va être encore les mêmes
pavillons qu'à Montréal il y a trois ans. La Tchécoslovaquie
avec sa 'Lanterna Magika' et tutti quanti. (. . .) Non, j'irais
plutôt voir un spectacle de bunraku, moi. Tu sais qu'Osaka
c'est la ville du bunraku? Enfin, c'est pas ici que ça a été
inventé mais c'est ici que ça s'est développé . . . À quelle
heure la pièce ce soir? Huit heures? [So we have to go to the
drugstore because I can't get through the day like this. I
have no desire to go to this expo this afternoon. (*A second
picture is taken.*) . . . It's going to be all the same pavilions as
in Montreal three years ago, anyway. Czechoslovakia and
its 'Lanterna Magika' and all that jazz . . . (*Third picture.*)
I'd rather see some bunraku. You know that Osaka is the
home of bunraku, don't you? Well, it wasn't invented here,
but it was developed here . . . (*Fourth picture.*) What time is
the show tonight? Eight o'clock?]

Walter   (. . .) Huit heures. [(*Coming out of the booth.*) Eight
o'clock.]

Patricia   Ça, par contre, je suis bien curieuse de voir ça,
cette *Dame de chez Maxim* . . . Un Feydeau, joué en français au
Japon par une troupe québécoise. Ça promet! [I can't wait to
see that, this *Lady of Maxim's*: a Feydeau, performed in
French in Japan by a Quebecois company. Sounds
promising.]

Walter   Laisse-leur une chance, Patricia, on n'a pas vu le
spectacle encore. [Patricia, give them a chance. We haven't
seen the show yet.]

Patricia   Non, écoute, je suis sûre que ça va être d'un
ennui! En plus, ils ont choisi la pire pièce de Feydeau! Ils
auraient pu faire *La puce à l'oreille, On purge bébé, Mais ne te
promène donc pas toute nue* . . . mais *La dame de chez Maxim,* c'est
mortel, c'est pas pour rien qu'elle est jamais montée. En plus,
tu sais qui a fait la mise en scène? C'est ce petit Français
chiant que j'avais connu chez Lecoq, Alexandre Haudepin
. . . À Paris, il donnait dans l'avant-garde, et maintenant, il
essaie de se faire une carrière dans le vaudeville à Montréal
. . . Écoute donc, Walter, c'est ben long ces photos-là. [No,

listen, I know it's going to be a bore. On top of that, they've chosen Feydeau's worst play. They could have chosen *A Flea In Her Ear*, or *Put Your Clothes On, Clarice*, but *The Lady of Maxim's*, it's deadly – there's a reason no one ever does it. And on top of that, do you know who the director is? It's that annoying little Frenchman I knew at the Lecoq school, Alexandre Haudepin. In Paris, he was in the avant-garde, but now, he's trying to make a career doing bedroom farce in Montreal . . . For God's sake, Walter, those pictures are taking a long time!]

Walter   Ça prend le temps que ça prend. [It takes the time it takes.]

Patricia   Bon, ben, écoute, je vais aller fumer une cigarette par là pendant que t'attends tes photos . . . [Fine, listen, I'm going to smoke a cigarette over there while you wait for your photos . . .]

Walter   Tiens, les voilà. [Wait, here they are.]

The pictures drop into the slot in the machine. He picks them up; she snatches them away.

Patricia   Mets pas tes doigts dessus, là, c'est pas sec, ça. (. . .) Qu'est-ce que je te disais? T'as l'air d'un clown, encore! [Don't put your fingers on them. They're not dry. (*She looks at them.*) What did I tell you? You look like a clown!]

They exit.

3: Feydeau

A gong sounds; music by Offenbach plays: the performance of Feydeau is underway. Technicians rush to perform a set change. They push a panel of doors onstage; we are looking at the backstage side of the doors, and observing the action behind the scenes of the production. Actors in period costume rush around, including **Sophie**, *who is wearing a chemise, pantaloons, high-heeled ankle boots, and her hair in a pile of ringlets. A dresser helps her into a corset.*

A technician helps **Hanako** *find her way into the translator's booth. She sits in profile to the audience. She is pregnant, and wears dark glasses. Her translation of the Feydeau is just audible to the audience.*

As the actors perform the Feydeau, we watch the action through the open doors. Recorded laughter plays during the scene. The technicians and the dresser remain visible to us during the scene, as do the actors who are not 'onstage'.

The scene concerns a **Monsieur Petypon**, *who has been dallying with a dancing girl from the Moulin-Rouge, called* **'La Môme Crevette'** *('The Shrimp Kid'), who is played by* **Sophie**. *The morning after their encounter, she comes back to get her dress, which she has left behind, and* **Monsieur Petypon** *is forced to hide her in the bedroom when his wife comes home unexpectedly.* **Madame Petypon** *finds the dress, thinks it's hers, and goes to try it on.* **La Môme** *appears from her hiding place and banters with* **Monsieur Petypon**. **Madame Petypon** *returns complaining that the dress does not fit, and* **Monsieur Petypon** *throws a carpet over* **La Môme** *and pretends she is a couch.* **La Môme** *pretends to make the couch come to life and convinces* **Madame Petypon** *that she is having a religious revelation. She tells* **Madame Petypon** *that she is going to father the man who is going to save France.* **Étienne**, *the* **Petypons'** *servant, comes in from an errand, carrying a lemon on a tray, and is forced to kneel and witness the 'revelation'.* **Monsieur Petypon** *says that the child could surely not be his, but* **Madame Petypon** *says this doesn't matter if it will help the country. They all declare 'Vive la France!'*

Note: This scene is an adaptation of a scene from Feydeau's The Lady of Maxim's *made by the authors of* The Seven Streams.

Petypon   Ah!

La Môme   Bonjour!

Petypon   Qu'est-ce que c'est que celle-là? Madame! Qu'est-ce que ça signifie? . . . D'où sortez-vous? . . .

La Môme   Mais comment, d'où que je sors? Eh bien! Tu le sais bien!

Petypon   Mais je ne vous connais pas! . . . mais en voilà une idée! Pourquoi êtes-vous dans mon lit?

La Môme   Comment, pourquoi que j'y suis? . . . Non mais, t'en as une santé! . . . Dis donc, eh. . . ! Il me demande pourquoi que j'y suis, dans son lit!

Petypon   Mais, absolument! Quoi? J'ai le droit de savoir . . . Qui êtes-vous?

La Môme   Non, mais on se croirait chez le juge d'instruction, ma parole! Qui que je suis? . . . Eh! ben, la môme Crevette, parbleu!

Petypon   La danseuse du Moulin-Rouge?

La Môme   Tu l'as dit, bouffi! On s'est pochardé tous les deux puis tu m'as ramenée à ton domicile!

Petypon   Moi, je? . . . C'est moi qui? . . .

La Môme   Dis donc, c'est bien chez toi!

Petypon   Mais, allez-vous-en, madame! On peut venir . . . Je suis un homme sérieux! . . . Vous ne pouvez pas rester ici! . . .

La Môme   J't'adore!

Petypon   Voulez-vous vous rehabiller! . . .

Mme Petypon   Eh! bien, quoi? N'importe! Chez l'épicier ou chez le fruitier . . . Vous avez de l'argent? Attendez!

Petypon   Ah! Mon Dieu! Gabrielle! . . . Cachez-vous! . . . Ne vous montrez pas! . . . Là-dedans!

Mme Petypon   Voilà le thé! J'ai envoyé Étienne acheter un citron.

Petypon   Madame Petypon! Ma femme!

Mme Petypon   Eh bien quoi?

Petypon   Madame Petypon, ma femme . . . Tu ne trouves pas qu'on étouffe ici?

Mme Petypon   Ici? Non!

Petypon   Mais si, mais si!

Mme Petypon   Mais non. Ah! Qu'est-ce que c'est que ça, qui est sur cette chaise?

Petypon   Quoi?

Mme Petypon   Cette étoffe? . . . On dirait une robe!

Petypon   Nom d'un chien! La robe de la môme!

Mme Petypon   Depuis quand est-ce là?

Petypon   Je ne sais pas! Je n'avais pas remarqué . . . Ça n'y était pas cette nuit! . . . Ce doit être une erreur! . . .

Mme Petypon   Mais pas du tout. Ce n'est pas une erreur. C'est la robe que j'ai commandée à ma couturière.

Petypon   À ta . . . ?

Mme Petypon   Mais oui, elle devait déjà me livrer cette robe hier.

Petypon   Mais non, ce n'est pas possible! . . . D'abord, je te connais, tu ne choisirais pas une étoffe aussi voyante! Allez, donne ça. Donne ça!

Mme Petypon   Ah! que tu es brutal! Tu as une façon de manipuler les toilettes.

Petypon   Eh bien! C'est du joli!

La Môme   Eh ben? Elle est partie? Dis donc! Tu m'avais pas dit que t'étais marié, toi! En voilà un p'tit vicieux!

Petypon   Oui! oh! Mais je ne suis pas ici pour écouter vos appréciations! Il s'agit de filer! Et vite!

La Môme   Ah c'est pas pour dire! T'étais plus amoureux hier soir!

Petypon   Oui! Eh bien! Je suis comme ça le matin! Allons, allons, dépêchez-vous!

La Môme   Mais tu m'as pas regardée mon petit père! J'suis habituée à ce qu'on ait des égards envers les femmes!

Petypon   C'est bien, on va t'en donner! . . . Combien?

La Môme   . . . Non, mais pour qui qu'c'est t'y q'tu me prends?

Petypon   Aha! . . . 'Pour qui qu'c'est t'y q' tu me prends?' Oh! non! qui qu'c'est t'y qui t'a appris le français?

La Môme   Quoi? quoi? Qu'équ' t'as l'air de chiner, toi? Eh! . . . bidon! Tu sauras que si je veux, je parle aussi bien français que toi!

> C'est en vain qu'au Parnasse un téméraire auteur
> Pense de l'art des vers atteindre la hauteur,
> Si le ciel en naissant ne l'a créé poète? . . .
> Mon histoire, messieurs les juges, sera brève! . . .

Petypon   Mâtin, du classique! . . .

La Môme   Ouais, du classique! Je suis de bonne famille tout comme tu me vois! . . . si je ne suis pas institutrice, c'est qu'au moment où j'allais passer mon brevet supérieur, je me suis laissé séduire par un gueux d'homme qui avait abusé de mon innocence pour m'entortiller de belles promesses! Tu comprends, il m'avait promis le collage.

Petypon   Oui! eh bien! C'est très intéressant, mais tu nous raconteras tes mémoires une autre fois!

La Môme   Ma robe!

Petypon   Comment ta robe?

La Môme   Mais oui, où est ma robe?

Petypon   Mais non, mais non. Tu es très bien comme ça! Va! File!

La Môme   Non, mais t'es complètement marteau? Tu penses pas que je vais me balader dehors en liquette.

Petypon   Eh ben! Je ne l'ai pas ta robe! Elle n'est plus là! Y en a plus!

La Môme   Où c't'y qu'elle est? Qui c't'y qui l'a?

Petypon   C'est ma femme qui l'a prise!

La Môme   Eh ben mon salaud! Donner ma robe!

Voice of Mme Petypon   Elle est folle, ma parole, cette couturière. Elle est folle! Je ne sais pas sur quelles mesures elle m'a fait cette robe . . . !

Petypon   Ciel, ma femme! Cache-toi! Cache-toi!

La Môme   Où? Où?

Petypon   Là! Là-dessous!

La Môme   Mais j'peux pas! Y a l'pouf!

Mme Petypon   Ah! Je suis épuisée! Asseyons-nous!

Petypon   Non, pas le pouf!

Mme Petypon   As-tu lu les journaux? Sainte-Catherine est apparue dernièrement, à Houilles, à une famille de charbonniers!

Petypon   Évidemment!

Mme Petypon   Oh! Ne fait pas l'esprit fort! C'est un fait. Il n'y a pas à dire que cela n'est pas! Et la preuve, c'est que je l'ai vue!

Petypon   Vous?

Mme Petypon   Oui, moi! Elle m'a parlé! Elle m'a dit: 'Ma fille! Le ciel vous a choisie pour de grandes choses! Bientôt vous recevrez la visite d'un séraphin qui vous éclairera sur la mission que vous aurez à accomplir! . . . Allez!'

Voice of La Môme   Gabrielle! Gabrielle!

Mme Petypon   Ah mon Dieu!

Petypon   Quoi? Quoi?

Mme Petypon   Vous ne voyez pas?

Petypon   Non! Non!

Mme Petypon   Voyons ce n'est pas possible! Je ne rêve pas!

La Môme   Arrête! C'est pour toi que je viens, Gabrielle. Prosterne-toi!

Mme Petypon Mon dieu, le Séraphin! À genoux! À genoux!

Étienne V'là le citron!

Mme Petypon Chut!

Étienne Eh bien quoi!

Mme Petypon Taisez-vous et à genoux!

La Môme Gabrielle! D'un pas rapide, tu iras jusqu'à la place de la Concorde dont tu feras cinq fois le tour. Puis, tu attendras à côté de l'Obélisque jusqu'à ce qu'un homme te parle! De cette parole te naîtra un fils! Ce fils sera l'homme que la France attend! Il régnera sur elle et fera souche de roi. Sur ce, à la prochaine! Moi, je m'évanouis dans l'espace et regagne les régions Célestes! Piouf!

Mme Petypon Parti! Il est parti! Place de la Concorde! Un homme doit me parler. De cette parole naîtra un fils! Et il sera roi, Lucien!

Petypon Mais ce fils ne sera pas de moi!

Mme Petypon Qu'importe, puisqu'il n'est pas d'un autre!

Petypon Mon Dieu! Qu'exigez-vous de moi?

Étienne Moi, si je serais à la place de monsieur, je dirais oui.

Mme Petypon Pour la Patrie!

Étienne Pour la Patrie!

Petypon Vive la France!

All Vive la France!

Blackout. The actors come 'backstage' (downstage, to the audience). The actors, who have been joined by two other actors, dressed as a priest and an upper-class woman, head 'onstage' for their curtain call.
Sophie *comes 'onstage' a little bit after everyone else for her bow, entering with a perky hop. The applause is enthusiastic; the actors run 'off' and then 'on' again for another bow.*

As they come 'backstage', the technicians change the set while the actors chat about how the show went. **Sophie** *doesn't seem very happy about it. As the rest of the actors head offstage,* **Sophie** *wishes them a good trip back to Montreal.*

4: La loge/The dressing room

A panel with a Western door in it has slid on stage left.

Sophie *remains onstage from the last scene.* **Hanako** *and* **Jeffrey 2** *enter. They speak in French, which is translated with supertitles.*

Sophie   Hanako! Bravo! [Hanako! Congratulations!]

Hanako   Bravo à toi! Tu étais vraiment formidable! Je te présente mon mari, Jeffrey Yamashita. [Congratulations to you. You were wonderful. I'd like you to meet my husband, Jeffrey Yamashita.]

Sophie   Bonjour! [Hello!]

Jeffrey 2 (*in English*)   Nice to meet you.

Hanako   Bravo, j'ai vraiment adoré travailler avec toi, vraiment, c'était un plaisir . . . [Congratulations. I really loved working with you. Truly, it was a pleasure . . .]

Jeffrey 2 (*in English, to* **Sophie**, *about the show*)   It was fantastic. Thank you very much.

Hanako   Tiens, je t'ai apporté un petit cadeau . . . [I brought you a little present . . .] (*She gives a package to* **Sophie**, *who opens it.*)

Sophie   Ah, c'est gentil . . . [Oh, that's nice . . .]

Hanako   C'est un masque de théâtre Nô. Le Nô est une forme de théâtre japonais très ancienne, j'ai pensé que ça te plairait. [It's a mask from the No theater. No is a very ancient form of Japanese theater. I thought you'd like it.]

Sophie   C'est vraiment gentil. [How kind of you.]

Hanako   Si jamais tu passes par Hiroshima, tu es toujours la bienvenue chez nous, ça me ferait vraiment plaisir de te recevoir. [If you're ever passing by Hiroshima, you are always welcome to stay with us. It would be a real pleasure to have you visit.]

Sophie   (. . .) Si vous venez à Montréal, if you come to Montreal, call me, OK? (. . .) Et puis tu m'écris pour me dire si c'est un petit garçon ou une petite fille? [(*To* **Jeffrey 2**, *in English*.) If you ever come to Montreal, call me, OK? (*Touching* **Hanako**'s *stomach; speaking in French*.) And you're going to write me, to tell me if it's a boy or a girl?]

Hanako   Oui, oui. [Yes, yes.]

Sophie (*in English*)   Goodbye, thank you very much!

Hanako *and* **Jeffrey 2** *exit, almost bumping into* **Walter** *and* **Patricia** *as they go.* **Patricia**, *aggravated, gestures to* **Walter** *that* **Hanako** *is blind.*

Walter   Je l'ai pas vue! (. . .) Mlle Maltais? [I didn't see her! (**Walter** *knocks on* **Sophie**'s *door and calls out.*) Miss Maltais?]

Sophie *comes out of her dressing room.*

Walter   Walter Lapointe, de l'ambassade du Canada à Tokyo. [I'm Walter Lapointe from the Canadian Embassy in Tokyo.]

Sophie   (. . .) Enchantée! [(*Shakes his hand.*) Lovely to meet you.]

Walter   Bravo, félicitations. Quel beau spectacle! [Congratulations! What a wonderful show!]

Sophie   Merci, merci. [Thank you, thank you.]

Walter   Laissez-moi vous présenter ma femme, Patricia Hébert. [May I present my wife, Patricia Hébert?]

Patricia   Bonsoir. [Good evening.]

They shake hands.

Sophie   Bonsoir. (. . .) Alors, vous avez passé une belle soirée, vous avez beaucoup ri, oublié vos petits soucis? [Good

evening. (*Pause.*) So, did you have a nice time? You laughed
a lot, forgot your little problems?]

Walter   Oui, on était très fiers! [Yes, we were very proud.]

Sophie   Le public japonais a eu l'air de beaucoup aimer ça,
ils étaient très enthousiastes. [The Japanese audience seemed
to enjoy the show, they were very enthusiastic.]

Walter   Oui, généralement les Japonais sont très timides,
mais ce soir . . . Je ne les ai jamais vus aussi chaleureux. [Yes,
usually the Japanese are very reserved . . . I've never seen
them so warm as tonight.]

Patricia   En général, ils raffolent de tout ce qui est
français. Oui . . . Et puis il y avait beaucoup de francophones
dans la salle. [They love everything French. Yes . . . And
there were many French speakers in the audience.]

Sophie   Tant mieux! [All the better!]

Walter   On a fait le tour des loges et il semble que toute la
compagnie rentre à Montréal mais que vous, vous restez ici?
[We went around to the other dressing rooms, and it seems
like all your friends are going back to Montreal tonight. But
you're staying?]

Sophie   Oui, je vais rester une semaine à Osaka et je vais en
profiter pour visiter l'exposition, les pavillons . . . [Yes, I'm
staying in Osaka for a week; I'm going to have a look at the
exhibition, the pavilions.]

Walter   Ah! Ben c'est parfait, ça tombe bien! On a fait une
réservation dans un petit restaurant japonais pas loin d'ici,
peut-être que vous pourriez vous joindre à nous? [Well,
that's perfect, we booked a table at a little Japanese
restaurant near here. Would you like to join us?]

Sophie   Oui, oui, oui, oui, oui . . . Y'a juste un petit
problème, c'est que moi et mon copain, on devait passer la
soirée ensemble . . . Peut-être qu'il pourrait venir avec nous?
Il joue dans la pièce . . . [Yes, yes, yes, yes, yes . . . there's
just a little problem. My boyfriend and I were going to spend

the evening together. Perhaps he could come along with us? He's in the show . . .]

Patricia Bien sûr. De toute façon, on a réservé pour douze personnes, alors . . . [Of course. The reservation is for twelve people, anyway.]

Sophie Ah, ça c'est dommage . . . [Oh, that's a shame . . .]

Walter (. . .) Alors est-ce que vous venez . . . [(*Gesturing to* **Sophie**'s *costume*.) Are you coming . . .]

Sophie Oui, je vais me changer, je reviens tout de suite. [Yes, I'll go change. I'll be back soon.]

Patricia Oui, d'accord. [Yes, OK.]

Walter Prenez votre temps! [Take your time!]

Sophie (. . .) Merci encore. [(*Going into her dressing room*.) Thanks again.] (*She laughs embarrassedly, shuts the door*.)

Patricia (. . .) Franchement, Walter . . . [(*She mimics* **Sophie**'s *laugh*.) Really, Walter . . .]

Walter Quoi? [What?]

Patricia Ben, tu trouves pas que t'en as mis un petit peu là? 'C'était fantastique, on est tellement fiers de vous. Le spectacle était magnifique,' gna gna gna, gna gna gna . . . [Don't you think you were laying it on a bit thick there? 'It was fantastic, we were so proud of you, it was a great show,' blah blah blah, blah blah blah . . .]

Walter C'était un très bon spectacle! [It was a very good show!]

Patricia Walter, c'était nul!!! [Walter, it was crap!!!]

Walter gestures for her to keep her voice down.

Patricia C'était nul, nul, nul, nul, nul, un des pires trucs qu'on a vus depuis qu'on est au Japon . . . Merci au théâtre québécois. (. . .) Ils ont un joli programme, par contre, hein . . . Mais, t'as lu les biographies des acteurs? [It was crap, crap, crap, crap, crap, one of the worst things we've seen in

Japan . . . thanks to the Quebecois theater. (*She looks at the program.*) Nice program, though . . . But did you read the actors' biographies?]

Walter   Non . . . [No . . .]

Patricia   Celui qui fait Monsieur Petypon, il a participé à plus de quinze créations collectives. Et il pense à l'instar de Cocteau que le métier, c'est ce qui ne s'apprend pas. Ça paraît! [The one playing Petypon participated in more than fifteen collective creations; like Cocteau he thinks the profession of theater can't be learned. So it seems.]

François-Xavier, *the actor who played* **Petypon**, *crosses behind them wearing his street clothes.*

Walter   Monsieur Petypon!

Patricia   Bonsoir . . . [Good evening . . .]

Walter   C'est pas votre vrai nom, ça! [That's not your real name!]

François-Xavier   Non, c'est mon personnage. [No, it's my character.]

Walter   Laissez-moi vous présenter ma femme, Patricia Hébert. [Let me introduce my wife, Patricia Hébert.]

Patricia   (. . .) Bonsoir, bonsoir . . . [(*She and* **François-Xavier** *shake hands.*) Good evening, good evening . . .]

François-Xavier   Vous avez aimé le spectacle? [Did you like the show?]

Walter   Oui, on a beaucoup ri! (. . .) Ah, ah, ça sera pas long, elle est en train de se changer, deux minutes. [Yes, we laughed a lot. (**François-Xavier** *heads for* **Sophie**'s *dressing room.*) She's just changing. Wait a minute.]

François-Xavier   (. . .) C'est moi. [(*Knocking on* **Sophie**'s *door.*) It's me.]

Sophie   (. . .) Bravo! (. . .) C'est François-Xavier, mon copain, qui jouait Monsieur Petypon dans la pièce . . . [[(*Coming out of her dressing room and embracing* **François-**

Xavier.) Congratulations! (*To* **Walter** *and* **Patricia.**) It's
François-Xavier, my boyfriend, who plays Monsieur
Petypon in the show.]

Patricia   Oui, on l'a reconnu. [Yes, we recognized him.]

François-Xavier   (. . .) T'es prête, on va à l'hôtel? [(*To*
Sophie.) Are you ready? Let's go to the hotel.]

Sophie   Il y un petit changement. Walter et . . . [There's a
little change in the plans. Walter and . . .] (*She can't remember*
Patricia's *name and snaps her fingers in* **Patricia**'s *direction.*)

Patricia   Patricia!

Sophie   Patricia . . . nous ont invités à souper et je me
disais que ça pourrait être agréable, les quatre, ensemble . . .
[Patricia . . . they've invited us to dinner and I thought it
would be nice for the four of us to go together . . .]

François-Xavier   Écoute, on avait dit qu'on allait à
l'hôtel, on avait à se parler! [Listen, we said we were going to
the hotel. I need to talk to you.]

Sophie   Mais on peut se parler plus tard. [But we can talk
later.]

François-Xavier   Non. Dans ce cas-là, on va se parler
tout de suite! (. . .) Excusez-nous . . . [No, we need to talk
right now! (*To* **Patricia** *and* **Walter.**) Excuse us.]

Sophie   Ça serait pas long. [It won't be long.]

Patricia   Prenez votre temps, là. (. . .) Franchement! . . .
Ils sont pas très polis! Qu'est-ce que c'est que ces messes
basses? Ah! la la, les joies de la diplomatie! (. . .) C'est elle ça?
Elle est jolie hein? Elle est . . . photogénique. Mais elle est pas
très bonne! [Take your time. (**Sophie** *and* **François-Xavier**
go into the dressing room. **Patricia** *tosses her head and rolls her eyes.*)
For God's sake! They're not very polite. What's all this
whispering about? Ah, yes . . . the joys of diplomacy!
(*Looking at the program.*) That's her there? She's pretty, eh?
She's photogenic. But she's not very good!]

Walter   Ben voyons Patricia! [Now look, Patricia!]

Patricia   Enfin quoi, elle a un joli minois, elle est bien plantureuse . . . mais cette voix qu'elle a, ce ton, traînard et nasillard . . . Moi, je trouve que son jeu est complètement pathétique, si tu veux mon avis. [Well, she's cute and she's got a nice figure, but that voice she's got – her tone is so drawling and nasal. If you want my opinion, her performance was totally pathetic.]

Sophie *and* **François-Xavier***'s raised voices are heard coming out of the dressing room.* **François-Xavier** *throws the door open and steps out; we can see* **Sophie** *sitting down with her head bowed. He shuts the door behind him.*

François-Xavier   Je . . . je vais pas y aller . . . [I . . . I can't come after all.] (*He shakes their hands.*)

Patricia   Vous ne venez pas dîner avec nous? [You're not coming to dinner with us?]

François-Xavier   Non, non . . . Finita la commedia! [No, no . . . (*In Italian.*) This show is over!] (*He exits with a dramatic flourish.*)

Patricia   Qu'est-ce qui se passe, là? [What's going on?]

Walter   Je le sais pas! [I don't know!]

Patricia   Bon, écoute Walter, on va annuler ce dîner! [Listen, Walter, you have to cancel this dinner!]

Walter   Non, on va pas annuler le dîner, voyons! [I can't cancel it!]

Patricia   De toute évidence, ils ont pas envie de venir . . . J'ai l'impression que le torchon brûle dans le ménage. Petypon s'est barré et la Crevette est coincée dans sa loge! [It's clear they don't want to come . . . I have the feeling that their relationship is on the rocks. Petypon cleared out and the Crevette is stuck in her dressing room!]

Walter   On va attendre qu'elle sorte de la loge, on verra après. [Wait until she comes out. Then we'll see.]

Patricia   Walter, on annule ce dîner . . . trouve une
excuse, t'es un diplomate ou quoi? [Walter, cancel this
dinner. Find an excuse. Are you a diplomat or what?]

Sophie *comes out of her dressing room. She looks very depressed.*

Walter   Est-ce que ça va? [Is everything OK?]

Sophie   Oui . . . Finalement il ne viendra pas avec nous
. . . il avait d'autres projets . . . [François-Xavier isn't
coming after all . . . He has other plans . . .]

Patricia   Oui, on a cru comprendre. Est-ce que vous venez
de toute façon? [Yes, we gathered that. Do you want to come
anyway?]

Sophie *nods that she wants to come.*

Walter   Alors . . . On y va? [Shall we go?]

They exit together, **Sophie** *walking dejectedly with her head bowed.*

5: Photomaton 2/Photo booth 2

The Osaka train station set returns. **Hanako** *is sitting in the photo
booth and her image appears on the screen stage right. As the light
flashes, she throws up her hand to protect her face; her image freezes.*

In the center panel, a video of an atomic explosion appears. When
Hanako's *image turns live again, she is putting her dark glasses on.
The light flashes and her image freezes again. The image goes live; she
and* **Jeffrey 2** *are sitting in the booth together. Freeze. The image
goes live;* **Jeffrey 2** *kisses her neck and they both smile and laugh.
Flash – freeze.*

*They come out of the booth together. The immediate departure of a train
to Kobe is announced. They look impatiently in the booth's slot for their
pictures, which are not ready, then leave hurriedly. A few seconds later,
the pictures drop into the slot of the booth.*

6: Le restaurant/The restaurant

*Technicians change the set to one of a private room in a Japanese
restaurant – a low table, a partition with a sliding door, and tatamis on
the floor. A Japanese waitress opens the door to reveal* **Patricia**,
Walter, *and* **Sophie** *standing outside the door, taking off their shoes.
The* **Translator** *appears in the booth stage left. The dialogue in this
scene is spoken in French with simultaneous English translation.*
Patricia*'s manner throughout the scene is bitter and cynical, while*
Sophie *is quietly angry and often distracted.* **Walter** *observes their
verbal banter bemusedly; he barely seems able to keep up.*

Patricia/Translator   Eh ben, heureusement qu'on n'est
pas douze. (. . .) Vous n'êtes pas si grande, finalement . . .
Sur scène, vous avez l'air très grande, mais habillée comme
ça, en civil, et puis sans les chaussures . . . Vous n'êtes pas si
grande que ça . . . [It's a good thing there aren't twelve of
us. (*To* **Sophie**.) You're not so tall after all. On stage, you
seem very tall, but in plain clothes and without your shoes,
you're not as tall as all that.]

Sophie/Translator   Je suis quand même plus grande que
vous. [I'm still taller than you.]

Patricia/Translator   Ça, c'est pas très difficile. Vous
avez pas de mérite. [That's not difficult. You don't score any
points there.]

They sit down at the table. **Patricia** *and* **Sophie** *face each other and*
Walter *sits facing the audience.*

Walter/Translator   Mon dieu . . . Vous devez être
épuisée, après une telle performance, hein? [My goodness,
you must be exhausted after that performance.]

Patricia/Translator   Pas vraiment hein? L'adrénaline,
ça nous tient encore pendant un petit moment. Je connais ça
un petit peu, j'ai fait du théâtre, déjà. [Not really, the
adrenalin will keep you going a while longer. I know that
myself a bit. I used to be in the theater.]

Sophie/Translator   Ça fait longtemps? [A long time
ago?]

Patricia/Translator   Ben, pas si longtemps que ça, je suis pas si vieille, mais quelques années, oui, quand je vivais à Paris. [Not as long as all that, I'm not that old, but a few years ago, when I was living in Paris.]

Sophie/Translator   Ah, vous êtes parisienne? [Oh, are you Parisian?]

Patricia/Translator   Non, non, je suis montréalaise. En fait, je suis à moitié française, ma mère est québécoise mais mon père était français. Alors, j'ai été élevée à Montréal, et puis ensuite, on est parti vivre à Paris . . . [No, no, no, I'm from Montreal. In fact, I'm half French, my mother was Quebecoise but my father was French. So I was raised in Montreal, but later we went to live in Paris . . .]

Sophie/Translator   Ah! c'est pour ça que vous avez l'accent français . . . [Oh! That's why you have a French accent . . .]

Patricia/Translator   Ah, vous trouvez? [Do you think so?]

Sophie/Translator   Ben! [Sure!]

Patricia/Translator   Donc, à la fin de mon adolescence, on est parti vivre à Paris et puis j'ai fait des leçons de théâtre là-bas. [So, at the end of my teens I went to live in Paris. It was there that I studied theater.]

Walter/Translator   C'est là qu'on s'est rencontré! [That was where we met!]

Patricia/Translator   Ouais . . . [Yes . . .]

Sophie/Translator   Vous avez pas eu vraiment envie de poursuivre? . . . [So . . . you didn't want to pursue . . .]

Patricia/Translator   Pas vraiment, non. Je n'avais pas vraiment la vocation. Comme disent les Anglais, ce n'était pas ma tasse de thé. Non, je pense que . . . je sais pas . . . peut-être que . . . l'aspect exhibitionniste de la profession me rebutait un petit peu. Et puis moi je préfère travailler toute seule. Tous ces trucs collectifs, ça m'emmerde un peu. La création est un acte essentiellement solitaire. [Not really. I didn't really have the drive. How do the English say it? It wasn't my cup of tea. No, I think that . . . I don't know . . . It was the exhibitionist side of the profession that turned me off. And anyway, I like to work alone. All that collective stuff bugs me. I think creation is a solitary act.]

Sophie/Translator   Ça fait longtemps que vous êtes au Japon? [Have you been in Japan a long time?]

Patricia/Translator   Presque deux ans . . . [Nearly two years . . .]

Sophie/Translator   Vous avez des enfants? [Do you have children?]

Walter/Translator   Non, malheureusement. [No, sadly.]

Patricia/Translator   Non, non . . . On peut pas tout avoir, hein, on peut pas avoir le beurre et l'argent du beurre. Quand on veut faire une carrière, il faut faire un choix . . . Vous en avez, vous? (. . .) Vous êtes jeune, encore. Vous en voulez? (. . .) Bonne chance! [No, no, you can't have everything, eh? You can't have your cake and eat it too. When you want to have a career, you have to make a choice. Do you have any? (**Sophie** *indicates she doesn't.*) Well, you're still young. Do you want children? (**Sophie** *indicates she does.*) Good luck!]

Patricia *is smoking.* **Sophie** *indicates to her cigarettes, which are sitting on the table.*

Sophie/Translator   Est-ce que je peux vous en prendre une? [Can I take one?]

Patricia/Translator   Oui, bien sûr! Mais vous devriez pas fumer, hein, c'est pas bon pour votre voix, là . . . [Sure. But you shouldn't be smoking – it's not good for your voice . . .]

Sophie *takes a cigarette and lights up. The waitress is kneeling next to* **Walter**.

Walter/Translator   Qu'est-ce que vous voulez boire, Sophie? [What would you like to drink, Sophie?]

Sophie/Translator   Du saké, puis de l'eau, je suis un peu déshydratée. [Sake, and a glass of water because I'm a little dehydrated.]

Walter/Translator   Toi, Patricia? [You, Patricia?]

Patricia/Translator   Vin blanc, s'il te plaît, chéri. [White wine, please, honey.]

Walter/Translator   Je crois qu'on devrait commander la nourriture tout de suite, il commence à se faire tard. Vous voulez voir le menu? [I think we should order food right away. It's getting late. Would you like to look at the menu?]

Sophie/Translator   C'est en japonais! [It's in Japanese!]

Patricia/Translator   On est au Japon . . . [We're in Japan.]

Walter/Translator   Si je commandais un assortiment de sushis et de sashimis, ça vous convient? [If I order an assortment of sushis and sashimis, would that suit you?]

Sophie/Translator   C'est très bien. [That's great.]

Walter/Translator   Et toi Patricia, qu'est-ce que tu veux manger? [And you, Patricia, what would you like to eat?]

Patricia/Translator   Non, je mangerai pas moi. J'ai des brûlures d'estomac, là, qui me reprennent, j'ai pas vraiment faim . . . [I'm not going to eat. I have my heartburn again. I'm not really hungry.]

Walter *orders from the waitress in Japanese.*

Sophie/Translator   Ah! vous êtes malade? [Oh, are you sick?]

Patricia/Translator   Non, ne vous en faites pas, ce n'est qu'un malaise passager . . . J'ai l'estomac un petit peu fragile. [Not really. It's just a fleeting discomfort . . . I have a fragile stomach.]

Sophie/Translator   Excusez-moi, j'ai perdu le fil . . . On parlait de quoi? [Sorry, I lost the thread. What were we talking about?]

Patricia/Translator   On parlait théâtre. Création. [We were talking theatre. Creation.]

Sophie/Translator   Ah! oui. Et qu'est-ce que vous faites maintenant? [Oh, right. What are you doing now?]

Patricia/Translator   Maintenant, je suis inscrite au doctorat en littérature, à l'Université de Montréal. Mais pour le moment, vu qu'on est au Japon et comme on est là pour quelques années, j'ai décidé de profiter de la situation et de m'intéresser un petit peu à la culture orientale. Alors, je fais des cours de langue et littérature japonaises, et puis je fais un peu de sumiyé, aussi. [I am doing a Ph.D. in literature at the University of Montreal. But for the moment, since we're in Japan, and we're going to be here for a few years, I've decided to take advantage of the situation and learn about Eastern culture. So, I'm taking classes in Japanese language and literature, and I do a little sumiyé, too.]

Sophie/Translator   Je sais pas c'est quoi . . . [I don't know what that is.]

Patricia/Translator   Ah! vous connaissez pas le sumiyé? C'est une forme de peinture, japonaise évidemment, un peu comme la calligraphie, mais ce qu'il y a de particulier, c'est que l'artiste doit atteindre un très, très haut niveau de concentration et puis tout à coup le trait jaillit, comme ça, d'un seul geste. (. . .) C'est très intéressant! [You don't know sumiyé? It's a form of painting, Japanese, obviously, a little bit like calligraphy. But what's special about it is that the artist needs to attain a very, very high level of concentration and then all of a sudden the gesture comes out in one stroke . . . (*Pause.* **Sophie** *is not listening.*) It's very interesting.]

Walter/Translator   Comme ça, vous passez la semaine à Osaka? [And so, you're spending the week in Osaka?]

Sophie/Translator   Finalement, non . . . j'ai changé mes plans . . . Je vais peut-être visiter le Japon . . . [In the end, no. My plans have changed. I'm thinking about seeing more of the country.]

Patricia/Translator   Oui, tant qu'à y être, il faut voir le pays un peu . . . [Yes, well you might as well, since you're here.]

Sophie/Translator   J'ai pensé à Kobe . . . [I'm thinking about Kobe . . .]

Patricia/Translator   Oui, c'est pas loin, environ trente minutes de train. La région de Kyoto, aussi, c'est très beau. [Yes, it's only thirty minutes by train. The area around Kyoto, too, is very beautiful.]

Their conversation overlaps.

Walter/Translator   Nara . . . Les temples . . . [Nara . . . the temples . . .]

Sophie/Translator   Ah! Nara c'est là qu'y a les, les, les . . . [Oh, Nara, that's where there are those . . .] (*She taps the fingers of one hand into the palm of the other.*)

Walter/Translator   Les daims. [Deer.]

Sophie/Translator   Les bambis . . . [Bambis . . .]

Walter/Translator   C'est ça, oui! . . . [Yes, that's it!]

Patricia/Translator   Les daims. [Deer.]

Sophie/Translator   . . . qui mangent dans la main. [That eat out of your hand.]

Walter/Translator   Est-ce que vous avez eu la chance de visiter Tokyo? [Did you get a chance to visit Tokyo?]

Sophie/Translator   Non, on a atterri à Tokyo mais il a fallu partir tout de suite pour Osaka, alors j'ai rien vu . . . [No, we landed in Tokyo but we came directly to Osaka, so I didn't see anything.]

Patricia/Translator   Ah! Bon, ben alors, écoutez, il faut voir Tokyo, c'est une ville fantastique . . . [But you have to see Tokyo; it's a great city . . .]

Sophie/Translator   Oui mais j'ai pas d'argent, je suis toute seule . . . [Yes, but I'm broke and I'm all alone . . .]

Patricia/Translator   Mais c'est très sécuritaire comme ville, c'est un des taux de criminalité les plus bas au monde . . . Et c'est pas si cher que ça . . . enfin, comme toutes les grandes villes . . . [But it's a very safe city. The crime rates are the lowest in the world . . . And it's not that expensive . . . Anyway, like all big cities . . .]

Walter/Translator   (. . .) Mais j'y pense, on a une chambre d'amis, on s'en sert pratiquement jamais . . . Ça nous ferait plaisir de vous y inviter pour quelques jours, ou toute la semaine si vous voulez! N'est-ce pas, Patricia? [(*Interrupting.*) I'm thinking – we have a guest room in our house. We never use it. We'd be delighted if you would come stay for a few days, or the whole week, if you want. Don't you agree, Patricia?]

Patricia/Translator   (. . .) Pourquoi pas? [(*Coldly.*) Why not?]

Sophie/Translator   Je vais y penser. [I'll think about it.]

Patricia/Translator   Oui, c'est ça, pensez-y. (. . .) Ah, la bouffe! Vous avez faim? [Yes, think about it. (*The waitress enters with the drinks and food.*) Oh, the food! Are you hungry?]

Sophie/Translator   Très. [Very.]

Patricia/Translator   Ça se comprend, après une telle performance! Vous aimez les sushis? [That's understandable, after such a performance. Do you like sushi?]

Sophie/Translator   Au début j'aimais pas vraiment les fruits de mer, mais je commence à aimer ça . . . [At first I didn't like seafood, but I'm getting used to it . . .]

Patricia/Translator   Après deux ans de toute façon, vous en auriez marre. [After two years, you'd be fed up, anyway.]

Sophie/Translator   Ah, vous n'aimez pas la bouffe japonaise? [Oh, you don't like Japanese food?]

Patricia/Translator   Ah, je sais pas . . . Je peux pas vraiment me faire à la cuisine orientale . . . peut-être que ça dépend de la façon dont j'ai été élevée, mon background européen . . . Pour moi, un repas sans pain, c'est pas vraiment un repas. Et puis le riz, c'est pas vraiment la même chose . . . et puis, en plus, j'ai besoin de beaucoup de fibres, moi, dans mon alimentation, parce que . . . enfin . . . j'ai un . . . un transit intestinal difficile. Par contre, je trouve ça très joli. Esthétiquement, c'est vachement réussi. (. . .) Les couleurs et puis les formes des sushis . . . alors avec les baguettes, comme ça, on prend un petit peu de ceci, et puis un petit peu de cela, et puis avec la sauce, on mange comme ça (. . .) et puis, c'est comme si on peignait – mais à l'envers! [I don't know. I can't get used to Oriental cuisine. Maybe it has to do with the way I was brought up, my European background. But for me, a meal without bread is not a meal. Rice is not the same thing. And I need fiber in my system . . . because I have irritable bowel syndrome. On the other hand I find it very pleasant aesthetically. (*She picks up the plate of sushi.*) The forms, the colors. When you eat it with chopsticks, taking a little bit of this and that, and then some sauce, and you eat like this, (*Demonstrating with the chopsticks.*) it's like you're painting – backwards!]

Walter/Translator   Dites-moi quelque chose, Sophie. Est-ce que ça vous trouble de jouer pratiquement toute nue? [Tell me something, Sophie. Doesn't it bother you to perform when you're almost completely naked?]

Patricia/Translator (*reprimanding*)   Walter!

Sophie/Translator   Pardon? [Excuse me?]

Patricia/Translator   Walter vous a demandé si ça vous trouble de jouer court vêtue? [Walter asked if it bothers you to perform half-dressed.]

Sophie/Translator   Hmmmm . . . non . . . [Hmmmm . . . no.]

Patricia/Translator   Non? [No?]

Sophie/Translator   (. . .) Non. Non, parce que c'est justifié dans la pièce, parce que c'est une danseuse . . . puis aussi, c'est une critique sociale, parce qu'elle est une couche en dessous de la société. Puis ça fait rire, alors pourquoi pas! [(*Hesitating.*) No, because it's justified in the play. She is a dancing girl. Also, it's a social critique because she's from a lower class of society. And if it's just for laughs, then, why not?]

Patricia/Translator   Ah ben oui, hein, si ça fait rire. (. . .) Donc, vos costumes vous ont aidée dans la construction de votre personnage . . . [Well, yes, if it's just for laughs . . . (*Pause.*) So, did your costumes help you to build your character?]

Sophie/Translator   Hmmmm . . . non . . . [Hmmmm . . . no.]

Patricia/Translator   Ah! non? C'est vrai que dans Feydeau y a pas tellement de psychologie. [No? Well, it's true, there isn't a lot of psychology in Feydeau.]

Sophie/Translator   Ben, quand même! [Even so!]

Patricia/Translator   Ah bon? Si vous voulez . . . [Well, whatever you like . . .]

Walter/Translator   Moi, je suis pas un critique . . . [In any case, I'm not a critic . . .]

Patricia/Translator   Ah! ça non. [Clearly not.]

Walter/Translator   . . . mais j'ai beaucoup aimé votre performance. Je voulais tout simplement vous dire 'Merci'. [. . . but I really appreciated your performance. I just want to say 'thank you'.]

Patricia/Translator   Bravo! . . . C'est joli ce que vous portez, hein, c'est peu, mais enfin, c'est très joli. Ça doit être difficile, par contre, de jouer avec un corset, je ne sais pas, je n'ai jamais vécu l'expérience, mais jouer sanglée comme ça . . . pour la voix, la respiration, la projection. Quand vous faites le pouf aussi, ça doit pas être facile, avec cette chaleur, et puis . . . [Bravo! It's cute what you wear. It's short, but it's cute. It must be difficult to act in a corset like that. I've never done it myself, but being all strapped in must make breathing and projection difficult. And when you have to play the couch, it can't be easy, with that heat . . .]

Sophie/Translator (. . .) Vous pouvez le dire, Patricia.
[(*Cutting her off.*) You can say it, Patricia.]

Patricia/Translator Quoi? [What?]

Sophie/Translator En général, quand les gens disent
bravo pour les costumes, pour les perruques, pour les corsets,
pour le pouf, ça veut dire qu'ils ont pas vraiment aimé la
pièce. [Usually, when people congratulate you for the
costumes, the wigs, the corsets, the couch, that means they
really didn't like the show.]

Patricia/Translator Ah! non non, j'ai trouvé ça
intéressant, j'ai trouvé ça . . . divertissant. C'est sans
prétention, et puis vous avez beaucoup d'énergie, vous avez
du panache, enfin . . . [Oh, no, no. I found it interesting. I
found it . . . amusing. It's not pretentious and you have a lot
of energy, a lot of panache . . .]

Sophie/Translator Mais qu'est-ce que vous voulez que
ça me fasse! Feydeau, j'aime pas ça! La Môme Crevette, la
Môme Crevette, elle me donne envie de . . . (. . .) euh, euh,
euh, OK? La mise en scène est nulle! Je peux vous le dire,
c'est nul. Le texte est nul, le décor est nul, les acteurs sont
nuls! (. . .) Vous êtes diplomate vous? . . . expliquez-moi
donc ça qu'on fasse venir un metteur en scène français à
Montréal, pour nous apprendre à parler à la française dans
une pièce française, et que c'est ça qui représente le Canada à
l'exposition universelle d'Osaka!? Je vais vous le dire, moi,
c'est quoi, c'est parce qu'on est colonisé . . . Ça me donne
envie de sacrer, (. . .) tabarnac d'hostie de calice de saint-
ciboire!!! À part de ça, même De Gaulle l'a dit 'Vive le
Québec libre, calice!!' [I don't give a damn! Feydeau? I hate
it! The Shrimp Kid, the Shrimp Kid, it makes me want to
. . . (*She mimes sticking her fingers down her throat and makes
throwing-up noises.*) The direction, it was crap! I can tell you, it
was crap. And we were all crap! And the text and the
scenery, it was crap! (*To* **Walter**.) You're a diplomat . . .
explain to me how you can bring a French director to
Montreal to teach us to speak French with a French accent
and to perform in a French play – and that's supposed to

represent Canada at the Universal Expo in Osaka? I tell you,
it's because we're colonized. It makes me want to . . .
(**Sophie** *swears in colloquial Quebecois; the interpreter replaces her
swear words with the word 'expletive'.*) 'expletive', 'expletive' . . .
It was De Gaulle who said 'Long Live Free Quebec!',
'expletive'.]

Long embarrassed pause.

Walter/Translator   Ben, je pense pas qu'il ait dit calice,
là . . . [Well, I don't think he said 'expletive' . . .]

Sophie/Translator   Excusez-moi, je suis fatiguée . . .
[Sorry, I'm tired . . .]

Patricia/Translator   Non non, ça va. Écoutez, vous avez
droit à vos opinions. C'est pas parce que Walter travaille à
l'ambassade, qu'on est là pour faire de l'embrigadement. On
n'est pas responsable des politiques culturelles non plus. Et
puis c'est pas parce qu'on vit aux antipodes qu'on sait pas ce
qui se passe au Québec. Le nationalisme, le FLQ, les bombes,
tout ça, on en a entendu parler . . . Ça existe ici aussi, vous
savez. Y'a un auteur, là, qui s'appelle Yukio Mishima, vous
connaissez? (. . .) Il vient de former une armée. D'extrême
droite! C'est un grand auteur, par contre, hein . . . Il écrit
des pièces magnifiques. Vous devriez lire ça, vous, une
actrice. *Les Cinq Nôs Modernes*, et puis *Madame de Sade* . . .
Comparé à Feydeau . . . Non parce que Feydeau, vraiment,
vous avez bien raison, hein . . . J'aime pas Feydeau, ça
m'insupporte! [No, no, that's OK. Listen, you have a right to
your opinions. Just because Walter works at the Embassy
doesn't mean we want to bring you over to our side. We're
not responsible for cultural politics, either. And just because
we live on the other side of the world doesn't mean we don't
know what's going on in Quebec. Nationalism, the FLQ,
bombs, we've heard about all that. That's going on here, too,
you know. There is a writer here, named Yukio Mishima. He
just formed an army, on the extreme right . . . Do you know
him? (**Sophie** *indicates that she doesn't.*) He's a great writer. He
wrote some wonderful plays, too. You should read them,
you, an actress. *Five Modern No Plays*, and *Madame de Sade* . . .

Compared to Feydeau . . . Because Feydeau, well, you're
really right about him. I really don't like Feydeau. I can't
stand him.]

Sophie/Translator   On a ça en commun. [We have that
in common.]

Patricia/Translator   Walter par contre, il aime ça, lui.
Mais Walter, il aime tout, il est fou de théâtre, alors, les
quiproquos et puis les galipettes, le cocufiage, le mari
trompé, l'amant dans le placard, ça l'enchante, il raffole, il se
marre (. . .) Ça doit pas être facile pour une actrice . . . de
jouer dans un truc auquel on ne croit pas. [Walter, on the
other hand, he likes all that. But Walter, he likes everything.
He's crazy about the theater, especially all that flirting and
giggling, and cuckolding. The cheated husband and the
lover in the closet . . . he finds all of that enchanting, he
adores that, it cracks him up . . . (**Walter** *shrugs*.) It can't be
easy for an actress, to perform in a show that you don't
believe in.]

Sophie/Translator   Ça arrive souvent, vous savez. On est
engagé pour jouer dans une pièce et puis qu'on aime ça ou
non . . . Mais il faut y croire, il faut faire semblant. Il faut que
je gagne ma vie, de toutes façons . . . [It happens all the time,
you know. You're hired to perform in a show whether you
like the show or not. But you have to pretend, you have to
make believe you do. I have to make a living, after all . . .]

Patricia/Translator   Ç'est un peu pour ça que j'ai
changé d'orientation d'ailleurs. Au fond, vous n'êtes qu'un
interprète. Vous êtes l'ouvrier, pas l'architecte. [That's part
of the reason why I went in another direction. In the end,
you're nothing but an interpreter. You're the worker, not the
architect.]

Walter/Translator   Patricia, si tu veux pas rater ton
train, il faudrait que tu y ailles tout de suite. [Patricia, if you
don't want to miss your train, you'd better go soon.]

Patricia/Translator   Quelle heure il est, là? [What time
is it?]

Walter/Translator   Il est déjà moins vingt. [It's already twenty to.]

Patricia/Translator   Oh la la, il faut que je file, moi! (. . .) Il faut que je rentre à Tokyo ce soir, j'ai une leçon demain matin et puis les trains sont tellement lents . . . [Oh, I've got to run! (*She stands up.*) I need to go back to Tokyo tonight; I have a lesson tomorrow and the train is so slow.]

Sophie/Translator   J'ai terminé, hein . . . [I'm done, so . . .] (*She starts to stand up.*)

Patricia/Translator   Non, non, non! (. . .) De toutes façons, Walter reste à Osaka toute la semaine. Il a des rendez-vous d'affaires . . . Donc, prenez votre temps, finissez les sushis et la saké, là, et puis, à votre santé, hein! [No, no, no! (*She gestures for* **Sophie** *to sit down.*) Walter is staying in Osaka for the whole week. He has business meetings . . . so take your time, finish your sushi and sake. To your health!] (*She takes a final gulp of her wine.*)

Walter/Translator   Est-ce que tu veux que je prenne un taxi avec toi jusqu'à la gare? [Do you want me to take a taxi with you to the station?]

Patricia/Translator   Non non, non . . . c'est inutile, je peux prendre un taxi toute seule. (. . .) Ça m'a fait plaisir de vous rencontrer. Et puis si vous voulez profiter de l'invitation de Walter et venir passer quelques jours à la maison à Tokyo, vous êtes la bienvenue. [No, no, no. There's no need; I can take a taxi by myself. (*To* **Sophie**.) It was a pleasure to meet you. And if you want to take advantage of Walter's invitation and come spend a few days with us in Tokyo, you're welcome.]

Sophie/Translator   Merci beaucoup. [Thank you very much.]

Walter/Translator   (. . .) Je vais être de retour dimanche soir. [(*To* **Patricia**.) I'll be back on Sunday night.]

Patricia/Translator   D'accord. Au revoir. [OK. Goodbye.]

They kiss goodbye; **Patricia** *opens the door and puts on her shoes.*

Walter/Translator   Au revoir! (. . .) Est-ce que peux m'asseoir ici? [Goodbye! (*To* **Sophie**.) May I sit here?]

Sophie/Translator   Oui, oui. [Yes, yes.]

Patricia/Translator   J'ai toujours peur que quelqu'un parte avec mes chaussures. J'aime bien les vôtres! [I'm always worried that someone will leave with my shoes. I like yours!]

Sophie/Translator   Laissez-les là! [Leave them there!]

Patricia/Translator   Ouais, ah . . . De toute façon, elles seraient un petit peu trop grandes pour moi. Au revoir! [Of course. They'd be a bit big for me anyway. Goodbye!] (*She slides the door shut.*)

Walter/Translator   Écoutez Sophie, je voudrais m'excuser pour les propos de ma femme. Non, non, non, je sais que parfois ses propos peuvent sembler un peu, ah . . . comment dire? . . . [Listen, Sophie, I have to apologize for my wife's remarks. I know that sometimes her remarks can seem a little . . . how to say it? . . .]

Sophie/Translator   Abrasifs? [Abrasive?]

Walter/Translator   Oui . . . Mais, voyez-vous, c'est pas par méchanceté. Elle a toujours rêvé d'être comédienne. Et lorsqu'elle vous a vue sur la scène ce soir, eh bien, son rêve s'est brisé! . . . Vous êtes tellement . . . bonne, vous êtes généreuse, vous habitez bien votre personnage . . . on y croit vraiment! Ma foi, il faudrait être allergique aux fruits de mer pour ne pas apprécier votre Môme Crevette. [Yes, but, you see, it's not out of malice. She always dreamed of being an actress. And when she saw you on stage tonight, well, her dream was broken! You are so . . . good. You are generous, you really live within your character; I really believed you! Indeed, you'd have to be allergic to seafood not to appreciate your Shrimp Kid.]

Sophie *simpers.*

Walter/Translator   Prendriez-vous encore un peu de saké? [Would you like a little more sake?]

Blackout.

7: Photomaton 3/Photo booth 3

The technicians slide the screens in front of the restaurant set. The **Translator** *clicks off his light and exits. The scene changes to the Osaka train station.* **François-Xavier** *is in the photo booth and a video image of his face appears on the screen stage right. His photographs capture him striking himself violently on the face. He exits the booth and waits for his pictures.* **Patricia** *passes him, running, realizing she's just missed her train. She stops short, throws up her hands, and swears.* **François-Xavier** *sees her and tries to avoid her, and leaves without picking up his pictures.* **Patricia** *paces near the photo booth, fuming, and sees pictures dropping into the slot. She looks to see if anybody is around, then picks them up and looks at them.*

Patricia   Oh, putain! . . . [Unbelievable!]

She exits the way she came.

8: Le ryokan/The ryokan

The technicians set up the next scene: When the doors are in place, the lights come up dimly behind the stage right panel; we see **François-Xavier***, in silhouette, holding* **Sophie** *in his arms; they both appear to be naked. Slowly, he lays her down on the floor and lays down on top of her. After a moment,* **Sophie** *stands up with a sheet around her and opens the door. She goes to the stage left panel, behind which there appears to be a bathroom. She goes in briefly, then goes back to the bedroom, slides open the door, and stands in the doorway; now it is* **Walter** *who is lying there, not* **François-Xavier***. Their dialogue is performed in French, translated with supertitles.*

Walter   Est-ce que ça va? [Are you all right?]

Sophie J'me sens pas très bien. Mais ça va aller. [I don't feel very well. But I'll be OK.]

Walter Il est quelle heure? [What time is it?]

Sophie Deux heures . . . [Two o'clock . . .]

Walter Mon Dieu, il est tard . . . je pense que c'est mieux que je rentre. [My God, it's late . . . I think I should go.]

He gets up and starts to get dressed.

Sophie Tu peux dormir ici si tu veux. [You can stay if you like.]

Walter Ah . . . J'aurais bien voulu rester, ce serait même très agréable, mais pour te dire la vérité, Patricia va peut-être m'appeler tôt demain matin et tu comprends, si je ne suis pas dans ma chambre, comme je la connais elle va se mettre à fabuler et puis à s'imaginer des choses, alors . . . [I'd really like to; it would be very nice, but to tell the truth, Patricia might call me early tomorrow morning and, if I'm not in my room, if I know her she'll start to imagine things.]

Sophie C'est la première fois que tu trompes ta femme? [Is this the first time you cheated on your wife?]

Walter Non, non . . . Mais je voudrais pas qu'elle l'apprenne. Je voudrais pas lui faire de peine. C'est parce que . . . je l'aime Patricia . . . c'est la personne que j'aime le plus au monde! Regarde, toi, t'as un chum . . . Ça t'empêche pas de t'envoyer en l'air. [No, no . . . But I wouldn't like her to find out. I don't want to hurt her. Because . . . I love Patricia . . . she's the person I love most in the world. Look, you've got a boyfriend and that doesn't stop you having a fling.]

Sophie On n'est plus ensemble. [We're not together anymore.]

Walter Depuis quand? [Since when?]

Sophie Ce soir. [Tonight.]

Walter Ah, je suis . . . je suis désolé, je savais pas. (. . .) Il faut vraiment que j'y aille. [Oh . . . I'm sorry, I didn't know. (*He is dressed and heading for the door.*) I really have to go.]

Sophie   Bye.

Walter   Bye. (. . .) Sophie, tu prends la pilule? [Bye. (*He goes to leave, then stops.*) Sophie, are you on the pill?]

Sophie   Oui . . . [Yes . . .]

Walter   Je demandais ça comme ça, là. Tu sais, on sait jamais . . . bye. [I had to ask. You know, you never know . . . bye.]

Sophie   Bye.

He exits, then rushes back again.

Walter   Ma femme, ma femme! [My wife, my wife!]

He runs into the bedroom and shuts the door. **Patricia** *enters, in a cold rage.* **Sophie** *turns away in disbelief.*

Patricia   Inutile de te cacher Walter, je t'ai vu. Désolée, j'ai loupé mon train. (. . .) J'attends tes explications. [Don't bother hiding, Walter, I saw you. Sorry, I missed my train. (*Pause.*) I'm waiting for an explanation.]

Walter   (. . .) Patricia, c'est pas ce que tu penses, elle s'est sentie mal au restaurant. Je me suis offert pour la raccompagner à son hôtel . . . [(*Comes out of the bedroom, groveling.*) Patricia, it's not what you think. She wasn't feeling well at the restaurant, so I offered to take her to her hotel . . .]

Sophie   Est-ce que vous pourriez discuter de vos problèmes de couple ailleurs, s'il-vous-plaît? [Could you discuss your marital problems somewhere else, please?]

Walter   (. . .) S'il-vous-plaît, Sophie, hein? (. . .) Merci! Et là, elle a été malade, c'est pour ça qu'elle est dans cette tenue . . . alors, j'ai appelé la réception pour avoir de l'eau chaude et du citron et quand tu es arrivée, je pensais justement que c'était le service aux chambres. [(*Tersely.*) Sophie! Please! (**Sophie** *turns away.*) Thank you! So, she's sick, that why she's dressed like that. I thought she should have some hot water with lemon, so I called Reception and when you arrived I thought it was room service.]

Patricia   Walter, que tu me trompes, passe encore, mais que tu me mentes! En plus, ton histoire est grosse comme le Titanic! Si tu penses que je vais avaler ça. (. . .) Tiens, ça c'est le service aux chambres, peut-être? [Walter, cheating on me is bad enough, but lying too? And it's as plain as the nose on your face. If you think I'd believe that story . . . (*There is a knock at the door.*) I guess that's room service.]

Sophie *opens the door.* **François-Xavier** *enters.*

Patricia   Ah! Monsieur Petypon! Entrez, entrez, bienvenue dans le club des cocus! [Ah! Monsieur Petypon! Come in, come in – welcome to the cuckolds' club!]

François-Xavier   Qu'est-ce qui se passe, ici? [What's going on here?]

Patricia   Tu veux savoir ce qui se passe? Je vais te le dire, moi! Mon cher François-Xavier, mon mari vient de se taper ta copine. [You want to know what's going on? I'll tell you. My dear François-Xavier, my husband just fucked your girlfriend.]

Sophie   J'suis plus sa copine. [I'm not his girlfriend anymore.]

Patricia   Oui, mais lui (. . .) il est encore mon mari. [Yes, but (*Gesturing to* **Walter**.) he is still my husband.]

Canned laughter plays. **Sophie** *looks up quizzically. Everybody else is oblivious.*

François-Xavier   (. . .) T'as baisé avec c't'hostie de bourgeois, d'opportuniste, d'insignifiant, de fédéraliste fini là?! [(*To* **Sophie**.) You fucked this bourgeois, opportunist, federalist nobody?]

Patricia   Je vous défends d'insulter mon mari. (. . .) Et puis en passant, ceci vous appartient! [I forbid you to insult my husband. (*Hands* **François-Xavier** *the photos.*) And by the way, these belong to you.]

Sophie   Réglez vos affaires, moi je m'en vais me coucher. [You straighten this out; I'm going to bed.]

*She goes to the bedroom and slides open the door. The doors of the
Feydeau set are there. She tries to open one, and can't. Canned laughter.
She runs to the other side and opens that door – more Feydeau doors are
in place. She opens one of the Feydeau doors, and* **Étienne**, *the
manservant from* The Lady of Maxim's, *enters with a lemon on a
tray, just as he did in the Feydeau.*

Étienne   V'là le citron! [Here's the lemon!]

*Uproarious canned laughter. The other actors from the Feydeau burst
on stage in their Feydeau costumes, join hands with* **Walter**,
Patricia, **François-Xavier**, *and* **Étienne**, *and take a bow
towards the audience.*

Enthusiastic canned applause and cheers. **Sophie** *joins in the bow
reluctantly, looking around her with increasing disbelief. The actors
run offstage and come back on for another bow.* **Sophie** *doesn't bow
with them; she slowly drifts down the stairs towards the rock garden
and makes her way to the phone booth, still wearing only a sheet
wrapped around her. The other actors exit.*

Sophie *goes into the phone booth and the light in the phone booth comes
on. The* **Translator** *enters his booth and clicks on his light. The
following dialogue is performed in French with simultaneous
translation.*

Sophie/Translator   (. . .) Bonjour, est-ce que je pourrais
parler à Madame Hanako Nishikawa, s'il-vous-plaît?
Madame Hanako Nishikawa. Hanako . . . Est-ce que . . .
[(*Shaken.*) Hello, could I speak to Mrs Hanako Nishikawa,
please? Mrs Hanako Nishikawa. Do you . . .] (*In English.*) Do
you speak English? I would like to talk to Hanako
Nishikawa, please. Thank you.

Hanako *appears in another translator's booth, stage left.*

Hanako/Translator   Moshi moshi. [Hello.]

Sophie/Translator   Hanako?

Hanako/Translator   Hanako desu. [This is Hanako.]

Sophie/Translator   Hanako?

Hanako/Translator   Hanako desu. [This is Hanako.]

Sophie/Translator   Hanako, c'est Sophie. [Hanako, it's Sophie.]

Hanako/Translator   Ah, Sophie! Comment vas-tu? [Oh, Sophie! How are you?]

Sophie/Translator   Pas très bien . . . Est-ce que je te reveille? [Not very well . . . Did I wake you?]

Hanako/Translator   Non, je dormais pas . . . Qu'est-ce qu'il y a? T'es malade? [No, I couldn't sleep . . . what's wrong? Are you sick?]

Sophie/Translator   Je me sens mal, je suis étourdie, je suis un peu perdue . . . [I feel bad, I can't get my head together, I feel a little lost . . .]

Hanako/Translator   Où es-tu? [Where are you?]

Sophie/Translator   Dans une cabine téléphonique. [I'm in a telephone booth.]

Hanako/Translator   Tu veux que je t'envoie quelqu'un? [Do you want me to send someone?]

Sophie/Translator   Non . . . [No . . .] (*She cries.*)

Hanako/Translator   Sophie? Tu pleures . . . [Sophie? You're crying.]

Silence. **Sophie** *cries.*

Sophie/Translator   (. . .) Est-ce que je te dérange? [(*Starting to calm down.*) Am I bothering you?]

Hanako/Translator   Non . . . [No . . .]

Sophie/Translator   Qu'est-ce que tu faisais? [What are you doing?]

Hanako/Translator   Je lisais . . . Je lisais des poèmes de Baudelaire . . . En ce moment je travaille à la traduction d'une anthologie de la poésie française. C'est très complexe parce que le langage est beaucoup plus riche que les documents que j'ai à traduire normalement pour le gouvernement. Alors parfois c'est difficile de trouver l'équivalence de certaines expressions dans une autre langue

. . . Par exemple, dans les textes de Baudelaire, il y a souvent ce mot: 'spleen', et puis en japonais il n'y a pas de mot pour dire ça. Cet après-midi, je travaillais sur des textes d'Arthur Rimbaud. C'est mon poète favori. Il a cessé d'écrire il avait dix-sept ans. Je trouve ça triste qu'il se soit tu si jeune. [I was reading . . . I was reading some poems by Baudelaire . . . I'm working on a translation of an anthology of French poetry. It's very complicated because the language is much richer than in the government documents I usually translate. So it's hard to find equivalent expressions in another language. For example, Baudelaire often uses the word 'spleen' and in Japanese there is no equivalent. This afternoon, I'm working on texts by Arthur Rimbaud. He's my favorite poet. He stopped writing when he was seventeen. I think it's very sad that he killed himself so young.] (*Or, at least, this is how the translator interprets* **Hanako***'s last statement.* **Hanako** *speaks now to the* **Translator**.)

Hanako   C'est pas ce que j'ai voulu dire. [That's not what I wanted to say.]

Translator (*in English*)   Pardon me.

Hanako (*in English*)   That is not what I wanted to say. (*In French*.) J'ai pas dit: qu'il se soit tué, j'ai dit: qu'il se soit tu. [I didn't say he killed himself, I said he went silent.]

Translator (*in English*)   I find it sad that he went silent so young.

Hanako   Traduttore, tradittore . . . Traducteur, traître . . . J'aime beaucoup la poésie française. Je connais pas la poésie canadienne-française . . . Écoute Sophie, je veux pas que tu restes toute seule à Osaka, pourquoi tu viendrais pas à Hiroshima? Demain, il y a un train dans l'après-midi. Je pourrais passer te prendre à la gare . . . [(*In Italian*.) Translator, traitor. (*In French*.) Translator, traitor. I like French poetry very much. I don't know French-Canadian poetry . . . Listen, Sophie, I don't want you to stay by yourself in Osaka, why don't you come to Hiroshima? There's a train tomorrow afternoon. I could come and pick you up . . .]

Sophie/Translator   J'aimerais ça . . . [That would be nice . . .]

Hanako/Translator   Je t'attendrai à la gare demain. Ça va aller? [I'll meet you at the station tomorrow. Will that suit you?]

Sophie/Translator   Oui, oui. Bonne nuit, Hanako . . . [Yes, yes. Good night, Hanako . . .]

Hanako/Translator   Bonne nuit. [Good night.]

Sophie/Translator   À demain! [See you tomorrow!]

She hangs up. Blackout.

9: Photomaton 4/Photo booth 4

Lights up on the set of the Osaka train station. **Walter** *enters, carrying suitcases, followed by* **Patricia**.

Patricia   Finalement, ils ont changé mon billet et ils ne m'ont pas chargé de supplément. Ils sont quand même courtois, les Japonais. Tu viens, là, parce que celui-là, je voudrais pas le manquer! [After all that, they changed my ticket without charging extra. They're very courteous, these Japanese. Do you have the suitcase? Let's go, because I don't want to miss that train!]

Walter   Oui, oui, Patricia. [Yes, yes, Patricia.]

They exit. **Sophie** *enters, wearing her minidress and carrying suitcases and a train ticket. She stops decisively and enters the photo booth. Her image appears on the video screen, and freezes as the first picture is being taken. In the second picture, she wears a different dress, as if time had passed by. In the third one,* **Hanako** *sits next to her. In the last one, both of them are making funny faces to the camera.*

They come out of the booth; **Hanako** *is no longer pregnant, but* **Sophie** *is pregnant. They hug.*

Hanako   Tu veux toujours pas me dire qui est le père? (. . .) Tu vas m'écrire pour me dire si c'est un garçon ou une fille? (. . .) Bon voyage! [You still don't want to tell me who the father is? (**Sophie** *indicates that she doesn't.*) You'll write and tell me whether it's a boy or a girl? (**Sophie** *nods.*) Have a good journey!

Sophie   Merci pour tout, Hanako! [Thanks for everything, Hanako!]

Hanako *leaves.*

The lights come up on the rock garden: No music plays and the No character is standing in the doorway of the telephone booth. He and **Sophie** *walk across the stage, countering each other as in the first scene of this section. They stop and turn once, as before, then turn and exit. Blackout.*

6: AN INTERVIEW
Hiroshima, 1995

1: Chinese story

A spotlight illuminates **older Jana** *sitting on the porch steps stage right. As she tells the story of 'The Loyang Beauty', it is played out behind the screens by three-quarter life-size puppets manipulated by actors wearing black clothes and hoods. Behind* **Jana** *stands another puppet that looks like her – it too has a bald head and wears a black robe. The story is accompanied by live percussion and music.* **Jana** *speaks in English.*

Jana   Once, in the days of the Song Dynasty, east of Loyang, a young girl was picking flowers by the river.

A puppet of a young girl appears.

She was a simple young girl with no mirror for her face. And above all women, she was the one the emperor desired, with a desire that shook the clouds and called for rain. That day, the emperor summoned his porters, and the convoy left by the country roads.

The emperor appears in a sedan chair carried by two servants. He sees the girl, stops his convoy, and talks to her; she shies away. He orders his servants to capture her; and the convoy leaves with the girl trailing behind, with her hands bound to the sedan chair.

Thus the beauty was taken, and along the road back, she did not raise her eyes. She was brought to the imperial palace.

A canopy bed appears center stage. The girl is brought onstage by two woman servants. They undress her and put her in the bed. The emperor enters and undresses; his body is withered and bony. He goes to the bed but the girl holds up a mirror to him; he recoils and sits down with his head in his hands.

The emperor had grown old. He who had once been the mightiest of men saw his pride wither before the mirror held up to him by youth and beauty. Thus the greatest joy gave way to sadness. (*Pause.*) The emperor's herbalists were commanded to devise an aphrodisiac for the young girl.

The canopy bed is flipped out of sight; underneath is a low table whose top is a glass, and which is lit from within so that the faces of people above it are illuminated. Two white-robed puppets – the herbalists – lean over the table holding vials and bottles.

From rare herbs, they had created some powders which they combined in their experiments. They exposed them to fire hoping this would yield a superior power. Suddenly a flame set off an astonishing clap of thunder.

A cymbal clangs loudly, and a long white cloth is waved over the herbalists' heads.

They had just discovered the secret of pyrotechnics. (*Pause.*) The herbalists invited the emperor to witness the fruit of their discovery. It was a lavish and colourful night.

The emperor enters and watches a fireworks show, represented by long red and white cloths which are waved in the air in time with the music of cymbals and gongs. The girl enters and watches the show. Afterwards, she beckons to the emperor and loosens her clothes provocatively. The emperor lifts her skirts and puts his head under them. She throws her head back as the lights fade on them.

By a twist of fortune, the quest for an aphrodisiac for the emperor's love had led the herbalists to invent gunpowder. And already, a weapon was taking shape of such power that it could conquer any enemy; a weapon that could strike at distance, mighty enough to bring an entire city to ashes.

2: L'interview/The interview

Jana *stands up and walks stage left, where a low table is set up and three people are sitting:* **Patricia**, *wearing a shorter hairdo than in 'Words' and a suit, and* **Régis** *and* **Nathalie**, *a film crew.* **Jana** *sits down at the table with her back to the audience.* **Patricia** *sits to her left, with her profile to the audience.* **Nathalie**, *the camerawoman, sits facing* **Jana** *with a camera on a tripod.* **Régis**, *the soundman, sits to* **Jana**'s *right and works a small sound board. There are tatamis on* *the floor and the screens are shut.* **Patricia** *speaks to the crew in French, which is not translated;* **Patricia** *and* **Jana** *speak to each other in English.*

Patricia   On est bientôt prêt, là? [Are you almost ready?]

Nathalie   Miss Čapek, could you look at Patricia, please?

Jana *does so.*

Régis (*to* **Jana**)   I'm gonna put . . .

Patricia   He's going to wire you, he is going to put a microphone on you. It's not the first time you give an interview, is it?

Jana   Oh no!

Patricia   You've been such a celebrity years ago, hmm?

The video camera turns on; a live video image of **Jana** *appears on the center screen. Throughout the interview, the audience can see* **Jana** *on the screen.*

Régis   Can you say a few words? . . .

Patricia   He wants to do a sound test. So if you could say a few words . . .

Jana (*to* **Régis**)   Do you like to listen to people?

Régis   Oui . . . I learn a lot of . . . things . . . Again, please . . . More . . .

Jana   J'apprends français quand je suis petite, mais j'oublie . . . [I learn French when I am young, but I forgot . . .]

Régis   Ça va pour moi. [That's OK for me.]

Patricia   Ça va? [It's OK?]

Régis   Il faudrait se dépêcher . . . [We should hurry up . . .]

Nathalie   Oui . . .

Patricia   On est prêt? [Are we ready?]

Nathalie   Il faudrait la poudrer, parce que ça brille . . .
[We should powder her, because it's shining . . .]

Patricia   Madame Čapek, if you don't mind, I'm gonna
powder your head, because it is shining . . . Don't worry, it's
gonna look very, very natural. It won't show at all.

Patricia takes a make-up kit out of her bag and powders **Jana**'s
scalp. **Jana** *laughs.*

Patricia   It's not the first time you're being made up, is it?

Jana   Oh no . . . But that's the first time that somebody
puts make-up on my scalp!

Patricia   Yes . . . It's rather unusual, hmmm? Can I put
some on your face also, because you have a slightly mixed
skin . . . (*Powders* **Jana**'s *face.*) And I won't put lipstick on
you, but . . . you can bite your lips and moisten them with
your tongue . . . (**Jana** *does so.*) Yeah . . . Fine.

Régis   OK. T'es prête, Nathalie? [OK. You're ready,
Nathalie?]

Patricia   Attends! [Wait!] (*To* **Nathalie**.) Tu prends mon
chewing? [Will you take my gum?]

She hands her chewed gum to **Nathalie**, *who recoils slightly.*
Patricia *speaks to* **Jana** *in an aside.*

Patricia   They're in training!

Régis   OK . . . Prêts? Alors, Jana Čapek, prise 1, ça roule.
[Is everybody ready? OK, Jana Čapek, take 1, we're
rolling.]

Nathalie   Ça roule . . . [We're rolling.] (*A cymbal sounds.*)

Patricia (*suddenly concentrated and to-the-point*)   Jana Čapek,
you had a childhood and a youth marked by anti-semitism,
war, seclusion and finally, exile. You then became one of the
most important artists of the post-war avant-garde, one of
the voices of the movement. What was it that brought a
European woman like you – Czech, a Jew, and above all, a
survivor of the concentration camps . . . My question is:

what led a woman like you to seclude herself in a zen monastery on the hills above Hiroshima?

Jana   You know, sometimes, one must let go of everything in order to gain anything. Many years ago, when I lived in Europe, it was fashionable to go into a dojo, and to sit in zazen, so I went. At that time, I did everything with excess: love, art, political statements . . . I was an angry woman who didn't know how to cry. Zen came into my life and I understood that if I wanted to find what I was so desperately looking for, I would have to make a choice.

Patricia   What kind of choice? . . . What were you searching for?

Jana   Myself, I suppose, as all artists and all human beings do. You know, at that point in my life, I was forty or so, I couldn't keep still. I had a fuzzy image of myself and I couldn't look at my reflection in a mirror. The image I saw was too troubled, tortured. Zen gave me some silence for the first time in my life. So, I shaved my sumptuous red hair and I started to find a new path. My zen master told me that zazen is also a mirror but that it stays pure. Illusions never tarnish it. As he said, the reflection is you but you are not the reflection.

Patricia   Ah, that's lovely . . . There is another zen saying: that tea and zen have the same flavor. You know the flavor of tea, bitter and sweet at the same time, but we Westerners have a more idealized vision of zen: peace, serenity, detachment, enlightenment, inspiration, all of that . . . But to spend twelve to twenty hours a day, meditating in that same position, and being struck on the shoulders with a stick when you doze off, being forced into this endless encounter with yourself, there's a pain in that. There's a suffering, isn't there?

Jana   Yes. I can even say that during the really first long meditations sitting in zazen, the pain is terrible! But you know, the body learns and the pain goes away. It's a discipline. But, the really deep suffering comes from the mind . . . You know, that consciousness of life, desires, the past or the future, that's the ego suffering. When the ego diminishes, so does the pain. That's what I've been working on for the past twenty years . . .

Patricia   Mmm hmmm . . . Speaking of pain . . . To have chosen Hiroshima, the city that is a symbol of pain, extreme pain, both physical and spiritual . . . Surely there are other zen monasteries in Japan and in China as well – you know, zen was born in India and then was adopted by the Chinese and was further developed in Japan – so, that you settled in Hiroshima, was it intentional or was it a coincidence?

Jana   I believe that Hiroshima chose me. Ten years ago, I came to visit a friend and I thought I would find devastation here, but instead, I found beauty. You know, that kind of silence after the storm . . . And I needed it so badly. I went to the Peace Memorial Park, and I found Prague! There, in front of me . . .

Patricia   How come?

Jana   You know the Atomic Bomb Dome?

Patricia   Yes . . .

Jana   It's built in a pure Prague Secession style!

Patricia   Really?

Jana   It was the only building at the epicenter of the bomb that remained standing . . . and the Japanese preserved it as a symbol of the war. It was designed by a Czech architect, Jan Letzl, who lived and worked in Japan during the twenties. So, for me, facing that metallic skeleton was like being in front of a mirror. This empty shell was myself. Me, with my illusions, and all my past that I carried on my old Jewish shoulders . . . So I understood that my place was here, in Hiroshima.

Patricia   But, Madame Čapek, you are not a ruin! Thank you very much, Madame Čapek!

Jana   Thank you.

Patricia (*breaks out of interview mode*)   Ça va? [Was that OK?] (*To* **Jana**.) Thank you very much. It was great! You were great!

Nathalie   Madame Čapek, so if you'd come here because the lights are already set . . .

Patricia   Yes . . . now we have to shoot the questions because we work with only one camera, so we have to shoot the questions to do the editing. It was very interesting . . . (*To* **Nathalie**.) Ici, ça va? Tu veux que je la regarde carrément ou tu veux que je triche? [Here; is this good? Should I look at her straight on or should I cheat?]

Régis   Patricia, fais attention avec tes mains . . . [Patricia, watch where you put your hands . . .]

Patricia   Oui, oui, oui!

Régis   OK, attention . . . Jana Čapek, contrechamp, prise 1, ça roule . . . [OK, Jana Čapek, counter-angle, take 1, we're rolling . . .]

Nathalie   Ça roule . . . [We're rolling.]

Patricia (*interview mode again*)   Jana Čapek, you had a childhood and a youth marked by anti-semitism, war, seclusion and finally, exile. You then became one of the most important artists of the post-war avant-garde, one of the voices of the movement. What was it that brought a European woman like you, a Czech, a Jew, and above all, a survivor of the concentration camps . . . My question is: what led a woman like you to seclude herself in a zen monastery on the hills above Hiroshima?

Jana   You know, my life . . .

Patricia (*out of interview mode*)   No, no, no, no, no, you don't have to answer!

Jana   I'm sorry . . .

Patricia   It's OK, we already have your answers, they were very good, we keep them . . .

Nathalie   Ça roule toujours! On continue! [We're still rolling! Let's go!]

Patricia   Oui, on continue . . . Alors, je vais faire la sortie, hein? [Yes, we'll go on. So, I'll do the ending?] (*Into interview mode.*) But, Madame Čapek, you are not a ruin! (*Out of interview mode.*) Je recommence, je recommence . . . [I'm going to start over, I'm going to start over.] (*Interview mode.*) But, Madame Čapek, you are not a ruin! A monument, perhaps, but certainly not a ruin! Thank you very much, Madame Čapek! (*Out of interview mode.*) C'est mieux comme ça, hein, c'est plus sympathique! [That was much better that way, much more likeable!]

Nathalie   Oui . . . Bon, on va faire des reaction shots . . . Oui . . . Souris . . . [Good, we'll do some reaction shots. Yes, smiles . . .]

She films **Patricia** *making different expressions.*

Patricia   Ça va? [Is that good?] (**Nathalie** *nods.*) OK, it's done. Thank you so much! (*To* **Régis**.) Oh, tu me fais un son d'ambiance? Tu enlèves le micro à Madame Čapek, hein, tu oublies pas? [Will you do a room tone for me? And take Madame Čapek's microphone off, don't forget . . .] Merci, Régis. (*To* **Jana**.) We are going to make a room tone, now, because if I have to do some editing in the film, I might need that . . . So we have to keep silent for a minute . . .

Régis *prepares a boom microphone for the room tone.* **Jana** *and* **Patricia** *stand up.* **Patricia** *takes a pack of cigarettes out of her bag.*

Patricia   Can we smoke here?

Jana   No.

Patricia   Oh! I understand perfectly. Well listen, I'm going to take one but I won't light it, OK? I'm just gonna suck on it. (*Showing her the pack of cigarettes.*) I gave up Gauloises . . . Because of the French nuclear tests, you know? . . . So I'm boycotting all the French products! It's disgusting what they're doing, don't you think so? You've heard about that, you watch the news? You read the papers?

Jana   Sometimes . . .

Patricia   I find it really disgusting . . . The same year as the fiftieth anniversary of the atomic bomb in Hiroshima, and they're doing nuclear tests in the Pacific . . . So, no more Gauloises, no more Chanel, no more Bordeaux, no more Camembert . . . until Chirac changes his mind, you know.

Régis   OK, Patricia, il faudrait qu'on aie le silence . . . [OK, Patricia, we need silence . . .]

Patricia   So, now we have to keep really quiet for one minute.

Régis   For everybody . . . OK, c'est parti. [OK, here we go.]

They don't speak for a minute. **Régis** *holds out the boom microphone and looks at his watch.* **Nathalie** *stretches out on the floor.* **Patricia** *fidgets and mimes talking to* **Régis**. **Jana** *stands quietly.* **Patricia** *looks around and notices the puppet that looks like* **Jana** *stage right. She goes closer and looks at it, intrigued.*

Régis   OK, merci beaucoup! [OK, thank you very much.]

Patricia   Well, it was very nice to meet you, very interesting . . . Would you like me to send you a videocassette?

Jana   Oh, sure!

Patricia   Do you have VCRs here?

Jana   I have friends who do.

Patricia   OK. So, as soon as this thing is over, I send you a cassette. Well thank you very much. Bye bye.

They all shake hands.

Nathalie   Goodbye!

Régis   Goodbye, thank you very much!

The crew leaves. **Jana** *closes the door behind them and goes to her table. Through the window she sees someone coming. She goes to the door and opens it; it's* **Ada**. *They embrace,* **Ada** *comes in, and they go offstage together.*

3: Le montage/Editing

Through the screens we see the herbalists' glass table in place. **Patricia** *is sitting at the table with one of the herbalist puppets. They are looking at the screen in front of them, on which is projected a video image of* **Jana** *talking, from the interview.* **Patricia** *speaks in French, translated by supertitles.*

Patricia   Ça manque un petit peu de relief, tu trouves pas, c'est un petit peu flat, hein? Moi je la trouve super intéressante, mais il me semble qu'il manque quelque chose . . . Et puis j'ai peur que le propos soit un peu hermétique pour le grand public . . . Je veux lui rendre justice, hein, elle était passionnante, cette bonne femme, je voudrais vraiment qu'on garde l'attention de l'auditeur. [It's lacking depth, don't you think? It's a little bit flat. I think it's really interesting, but it's missing something . . . And I'm also afraid the subject might be a little inaccessible to the average audience . . . I want to do her justice; she was so fascinating, this woman. I really want this to hold the audience's attention.]

There is a burst of cymbals and light; a long white cloth waves over **Patricia**'s *head.*

Patricia   J'ai une idée. On va illustrer tout ça un peu là, on va mettre des images, hein. Tu vas me faire une recherche, tu vas essayer de me trouver des documents d'époque, le dôme de la bombe A, si possible avant et après l'explosion atomique, et puis on va faire une super sortie comme ça, on va faire: fondu enchaîné, le dôme de la bombe A sur le crâne de Madame Čapek! Bon, écoute, je te laisse avec ça, moi il faut que je passe voir le patron, et puis ensuite il faut que je file à la maison parce que Walter m'attend, donc, on continue ça demain matin, hein? Bye! [I have an idea. We

could illustrate it; we could put images in. Do some research
for me. Find me some documents from that era – the A-bomb
dome, if possible before and after the atomic explosion. Then
we could superimpose the A-bomb dome on Mrs Čapek's
head! Good, listen, I'll leave you with that; I have to go see
the boss, and then I have to run home because Walter is
waiting for me. So we'll continue with this tomorrow
morning, eh? Bye!]

She exits.

4: Walter et Patricia/Walter and Patricia

The canopy bed from the puppet show appears.

Walter *enters, attended by the servant puppets from the puppet show.
As they flutter around him, chimes sound as they did in the puppet show.
The puppets take his briefcase from him; as he undresses, they take his
clothes. In his boxer shorts, he climbs into bed. A puppet servant brings
him a newspaper.* **Patricia** *enters. They speak in French, translated
by supertitles.*

Patricia   Salut! [Hi.]

Walter   Salut! [Hi.]

Patricia   Ça va? [How are you?]

Walter   Oui. Toi, ça va? [Fine, and you?]

Patricia   Non, ça va très mal. (. . .) J'ai bossé comme une
malade sur mon montage toute la journée et puis là, je viens
d'apprendre qu'ils veulent pas diffuser mon documentaire.
Je suis vraiment furieuse. En plus, je suis complètement
crevée, j'ai une de ces migraines . . . [Not fine at all. (*She is
getting undressed.*) I worked like a dog all day on my editing
and now they don't want to air my documentary. I'm really
furious. And what's more, I'm completely exhausted and I
have one of those migraines.]

A servant brings her some pills and a glass of water.

Walter   Allez, viens te coucher. [Come to bed.]

Patricia   (. . .) Ah, on s'accroche toujours les pieds dans cette latte de bois! (. . .) Il faut encore que je me lève aux aurores demain, il faut que je continue à travailler, je vais encore être bouffie comme une vieille pocharde . . . [(*She does a take as she walks across the floor.*) I'm always stepping on that broken floorboard! (*She gets into bed; a servant brings her wet tea-bags which she puts on her eyes.*) I need to get up at the crack of dawn tomorrow morning to keep on working; I'm going to be puffy like an old drunkard.]

Walter   Tu travailles demain matin? [You're working tomorrow morning?]

Patricia   (. . .) Oui, oui, je travaille! Il faut que je finisse mon truc, là. J'ai demandé à mon assistante de me faire une recherche, je vais peut-être réussir à sauver mon film . . . [(*Gives the tea-bags back to the servant.*) Yes, I'm working! I have to finish my project. I told my assistant to do some research; maybe I can save my film . . .]

Walter   Patricia, c'est samedi demain! [Patricia, it's Saturday tomorrow!]

Patricia   Ben oui, mais qu'est-ce que tu veux que ça me fasse? [Yes, but what does that matter?]

Walter   Je pensais qu'on passerait la journée ensemble . . . On se voit jamais! [I thought we were going to spend the day together. We never see each other.]

Patricia   Oh . . . Ben je sais bien qu'on se voit jamais mais qu'est-ce que tu veux, il faut que je travaille, j'ai pas le choix! [Oh . . . well, I know we never see each other, but what can I do, I have to work. I don't have any choice!]

Walter   Tu travailles trop Patricia, c'est pour ça que t'es tendue. [You work too much, Patricia, that's why you're so tense.]

Patricia   Je sais, je sais, je sais . . . J'suis tendue, j'suis tendue, j'suis tendue, puis j'suis déprimée en plus! [I know, I know, I know . . . I'm tense, I'm tense, I'm tense, and on top of that I'm depressed.]

Walter   Écoute, j'ai une bonne nouvelle! Ça va peut-être te remonter le moral . . . [Listen, I have good news. It might cheer you up.]

Patricia   Ben écoute, va toujours . . . [OK, tell me.]

Walter   On m'envoie en mission diplomatique en Chine pour deux ans! [They're sending me on a diplomatic mission to China for two years.]

Patricia   Où? [Where?]

Walter   En Chine. [To China.]

Patricia   En Chine-Chine ou en Chine-Hong Kong? [To China-China or to China-Hong Kong?]

Walter   En Chine-Chine. [To China-China.]

Patricia   En Chine-Beijing? [To China-Beijing?]

Walter   Shanghaï! Au consulat de Shanghaï. Le gouvernement canadien veut réorganiser tout le réseau diplomatique, en vue de la restitution de Hong Kong à la Chine Populaire. [To Shanghai! To the consulate. The government wants to reorganize the entire Canadian diplomatic network to prepare for the return of Hong Kong to China.]

Patricia   Et tu t'en vas en Chine pour deux ans? [So you're going to China for two years?]

Walter   Toi aussi, Patricia. Tu viens avec moi. Je me sépare pas de toi pendant deux ans, certain! [You too, Patricia. You're coming with me. I can't be away from you for two years, that's for sure.]

Patricia   Ben voyons, Walter! Moi, non, moi je vais pas en Chine. [But, Walter! I can't go to China.]

Walter   Ben pourquoi pas? [Why not?]

Patricia   Non, écoute Walter, je peux pas aller en Chine! Voyons, à quoi tu penses? Je suis en train de faire un documentaire antinucléaire pour le cinquantième anniversaire de la bombe atomique à Hiroshima; en plus, je suis personnellement farouchement antinucléaire; en ce moment, je boycotte tous les produits français à cause des tests dans le Pacifique, et tu penses que je vais aller passer deux ans avec toi dans un pays qui a refusé de signer le moratoire antinucléaire! Hein? Voyons donc, Walter, ça tient pas debout! La Chine en plus! Les droits de l'homme bafoués, la condition de la femme, les horreurs dans les orphelinats, les petits bébés filles qu'on jette à la rivière . . . Non, non, non! Non, non, non, Walter, je peux pas . . . [Walter, I can't go to China. What are you thinking? I'm making an anti-nuclear documentary for the fiftieth anniversary of the bombing of Hiroshima. And, more than that, personally, I am fiercely anti-nuclear, and I'm boycotting all French products at the moment because of their testing in the Pacific, and you think that I am going to go spend two years in a country that refuses to observe the nuclear moratorium? Walter, that doesn't hold water! And China, on top of everything. Human rights scoffed at, the condition of women, the horrors in orphanages, little baby girls thrown in the river . . . no, no, no! No, no, no, Walter, I can't!]

Walter   Calme-toi, calme-toi, Patricia! [Calm down, Patricia!]

Patricia   Je suis très calme. [I am very calm.]

Walter   On va se coucher, là, on va prendre le temps d'y penser puis on en reparlera demain matin. [We should go to bed. We'll take some time to think and talk about it again tomorrow.]

Patricia   Non Walter, on en reparlera pas demain matin, c'est tout pensé, moi je ne mets pas les pieds en Chine! [No, Walter, we will not talk about this again tomorrow morning. There's nothing to think about. I will not set foot in China.]

Walter   (. . .) Chut, chut . . . Relaxe-toi un peu, regarde là, on est bien, là, hein . . . Il faut pas que tu voies seulement le côté négatif, là. Tu sais, c'est une promotion pour moi, ça veut dire une augmentation de salaire, une plus grosse maison avec des serviteurs, une limousine . . . [(*Caressing* *her.*) Shh . . . shh . . . relax a little bit. Look, everything's fine. You need to look on the bright side. You know, it's a promotion for me. It will mean a big raise, a bigger house with lots of servants, a limousine . . .]

Patricia Walter, mais voyons, tu es de plus en plus bourgeois, t'as aucune conviction politique, t'as aucune intégrité! [Walter, you are getting so bourgeois. You haven't got a single political conviction, no integrity at all!]

Walter C'est à ton bonheur que je pense, Patricia! [I'm thinking of your happiness, Patricia!]

Patricia Ah, à d'autres! Mon bonheur, il est ici, Walter, c'est mon boulot! [Don't bother! My happiness is here, Walter, with my work!]

Walter Écoute . . . Hein, pense à ça, le premier juillet 97, ça va être un moment historique! On a raté la chute du mur de Berlin mais cette fois-ci, on va être aux premières loges! Il parait qu'il va y avoir le plus gros feu d'artifice de l'histoire de l'humanité! [Listen, think about this: the 1st of July 1997 is going to be a historic moment! We missed the fall of the Berlin Wall, but this time we're going to be in the front row! It looks like they're going to have the largest fireworks show in human history.]

Patricia Écoute, si tu penses que tu vas m'avoir avec un feu d'artifice, j'ai passé l'âge, j'ai plus douze ans! [Look, if you think you're going to buy me with a fireworks show . . . I'm not twelve years old anymore!]

Walter Bon, bon, bon . . . Hein, on va dormir un petit peu . . . [Fine, fine, fine . . . let's go to sleep.]

Patricia Oui, Walter, il faut que je dorme. [Yes, Walter, I have to sleep.]

Walter Ooouuii . . . Il faut que tu te relaxes, aussi, hein . . . [Yes, and you need to relax, too.]

Patricia Oui, oui, oui . . . [Yes, yes, yes . . .]

They lie down, and he starts to caress her.

Walter   Hmmmm Patricia . . . Est-ce qu'on va faire un tour sur la grande muraille de Chine? [Hmmm, Patricia . . . do you want to take a walk on the Great Wall of China?]

Patricia   Ah vraiment, Walter . . . T'es ridicule! (. . .) Ah Walter, franchement! [Oh, really, Walter, you're ridiculous! (*He keeps touching her*.) Really, Walter!]

Walter   (. . .) Est-ce qu'on va faire un tour dans la Cité Interdite? [(*Running his hands down her body*.) Shall we go to the Forbidden City?]

Patricia   Walter, t'es grotesque! Arrête, là, j'ai pas envie, arrête! [Walter, you're grotesque! Stop it! I'm not in the mood!]

Walter   Ah, Patricia, ça fait longtemps, là . . . [Oh, Patricia, it's been a long time . . .]

Patricia   Oui, je sais que ça fait longtemps. (. . .) Walter! Walter, laisse-moi tranquille, ça me le dit pas! Fous-moi la paix! [Yes, I know it's been a long time. (*He puts his arms around her and kisses her*.) Walter! Leave me alone! I'm not in the mood. Leave me in peace!]

Walter   (. . .) Bon, bon, bon! (. . .) Tu veux avoir la paix, tu vas l'avoir, la paix! [(*He jumps out of bed*.) Fine, fine, fine! (*He starts putting on his clothes, brought to him by the puppet servants*.) You want peace, you can have peace!]

Patricia   Qu'est-ce que tu fais? [What are you doing?]

A servant brings the phone; **Walter** *takes it.*

Walter (*into the phone*)   Ma limousine! (*In English*.) The car, please, right now!

Patricia   Walter, où tu vas? [Walter, where are you going?]

Walter   Je m'en vais au bureau! [I'm going to the office!]

Patricia   Ben voyons, c'est le milieu de la nuit! [But it's the middle of the night!]

Walter   Je m'en fous que ça soit le milieu de la nuit! Je vais faire comme les Japonais, je vais travailler de jour comme de nuit! [I am well aware that it's the middle of the night. I'm going to be like the Japanese. I'm going to work day and night.]

Patricia   Walter, franchement, t'es ridicule . . . [Walter, really, you're ridiculous.]

Walter   Je suis pas ridicule! je vais devenir un workaholic, comme toi, Patricia. Parce que c'est ça que t'es, toi, une workaholic! [I am not ridiculous. I'm going to become a workaholic, Patricia, like you, because that's what you are – you're a workaholic.]

Patricia   Ben voyons, Walter . . . je suis pas workaholic, j'aime mon métier, c'est différent! [Look, Walter . . . I'm not a workaholic, I love my job, there's a difference!]

Walter   Tu travailles tout le temps, on se voit jamais. [You work all the time, we never see each other.]

Patricia   On se voit là, et tu fais que gueuler . . . [Well we're seeing each other now and all you can do is quarrel.]

Walter   (. . .) On se voit cinq minutes par jour, et t'es toujours fatiguée, toujours de mauvaise humeur, toujours en train de dire non, non pas ce soir, non pas maintenant, non pas demain . . . Avant, on faisait des choses ensemble, on avait des projets, on avait une vie, mais maintenant, même passer une journée ensemble, c'est trop te demander! Tu veux même plus faire l'amour avec moi! Ça existe plus, notre couple, Patricia! Veux-tu bien me dire pourquoi on est encore ensemble? Qu'est-ce qui nous retient? Si au moins on avait eu des enfants, mais non, t'as jamais voulu en avoir, t'avais peur que ça prenne trop de place dans ta vie, alors on a fait comme d'habitude, on a fait comme t'as voulu, Patricia! On a toujours fait ce que tu voulais, c'est toujours toi qui as tout décidé! [(*Very upset.*) We see each other for five minutes a day, and you're always exhausted, always in a bad mood, always saying no, not this evening, not now, not tomorrow . . . We used to do things together before, we made plans, we had a life, but now, even to spend a day together is too much to ask! You don't even want to make love anymore! As a couple, we no longer exist, Patricia! Just tell me why we are still together. What's keeping us together? At least if we had children, but no, you don't want any, you're afraid they would take up too much space in your life, so as usual we do what you want, Patricia! We've always done what you want, it's always you who decides everything!]

Patricia   (. . .) Ça c'est faux, Walter, moi j'ai sacrifié ma carrière d'actrice pour te suivre au Japon, mais là, j'abandonnerai pas mon métier de journaliste pour t'accompagner dans un pays dont la politique va à l'encontre de toutes mes convictions! [(*Exploding.*) That's not true, Walter, I've sacrificed my career as an actress to go with you to Japan, but I'm not going to give up my career as a journalist to follow you to a country with politics that go against all my convictions!]

Walter   Justement! T'as le choix, Patricia. C'est ta job, ou c'est moi. Tu viens en Chine avec moi, ou je divorce! [Exactly! It's your choice, Patricia. Your job or me. Either you come to China with me or we get a divorce!]

Patricia   Tu dis vraiment n'importe quoi! [You're talking nonsense!]

Walter   Patricia, je suis très sérieux! Choisis: c'est la Chine ou le divorce! (. . .) Vas-tu la faire réparer, la maudite latte, tabarnac?! [Patricia, I am very serious. Choose: China or divorce. (*Dressed now, he goes to exit.*) Could you please have that fucking floorboard repaired, for Christ's sake!]

He leaves. **Patricia** *sits up in bed.*

Patricia   Walter! Walter! (. . .) Ah, ça suffit! [Walter! Walter! (*A puppet servant has come in with a drill and is fixing the floorboard. To the servant.*) That's enough!]

She crosses her legs with difficulty, yoga-style, and tries to meditate. She shuts her eyes; unseen hands lift her up so that she seems to be levitating. She cries out in surprise. She disappears through the back curtain of the bed. Blackout.

5: La limousine/The limousine

Lights up on the young woman puppet, who enters just as in the story of 'The Loyang Beauty', accompanied by the music from that section. The sedan chair enters, carried by the servants, but it's **Walter** *inside. He sees the young girl, and stops the chair. He calls her over and whispers to her; she shows him through gestures the costs of various sexual acts. He hands her the cord which tied the hands of the Loyang Beauty. She strikes him with the cord; he feigns fear. She ties up his hands and drags the sedan chair offstage. The puppet servants flutter along behind. Blackout.*

6: La marionnette vivante/The living puppet

Live video of **Jana**'s *face appears on the face of the* **Jana**-*like puppet that still stands stage right.* **Patricia** *enters, crosses to the puppet, and sits down next to it. She is subdued and thoughtful; she seems to be searching for something. The puppet starts to speak.*

Jana   The really deep suffering comes from the mind. You know . . . that consciousness of life, desires, the past or the future. That's the ego suffering. When the ego diminishes, so does the pain. Sometimes, one must let go of everything in order to gain anything.

Patricia *passes her hand over the puppet's face and* **Jana**'s *image disappears. Blackout.*

7: Le feu d'artifice/The fireworks show

Projection: 'HONG KONG, 1997'.

The national anthem of China plays. Behind the screens, **Walter** *enters and waves to unseen people. He stands with his back to the audience and watches the fireworks show, performed by the puppeteers as in 'The Loyang Beauty'. Afterwards,* **Walter** *applauds, then stands alone and silent for a few moments. Blackout.*

7: THUNDER
Hiroshima, 1997

1: Le bail/The lease

*Lights up on the inside of the house. The doors are closed but two people are visible inside, as is the kimono, hung up as in 'Moving Pictures'. Japanese music plays. A young man, **Pierre Maltais**, enters and walks onto the porch. We can see him in silhouette; he is carrying a big backpack, which he drops on the porch. He is clearly lost. He goes to knock, changes his mind, and trips over his backpack as he goes. One of the doors opens and **Walter** comes out. They speak in French, translated with supertitles.*

Walter   Pierre?

Pierre   Monsieur Lapointe? . . .

Walter   Pierre Maltais.

Pierre   (. . .) Oui . . . Ah! je suis vraiment content de vous voir. Je suis désolé, j'ai eu des problèmes à l'aéroport . . . l'enfer! [(*Goes to shake his hand.*) Yes. I am so glad to see you! I'm sorry, I had problems at the airport. It was hell!]

Walter   J'étais inquiet. Pourquoi n'as-tu pas téléphoné? [I was worried. Why didn't you call?]

Pierre   Mais j'ai essayé de téléphoner . . . Ça prenait une carte, les instructions étaient en japonais . . . J'avais juste des yen en papier. Je suis vraiment en retard? [But I tried to call . . . it took a card, the instructions were in Japanese . . . I only had yen in bills. Am I really late?]

Walter   Trois heures. [Three hours.]

Pierre   Merde! [Shit!]

Walter   Viens, viens, je vais te présenter. (. . .) Hanako, je te présente Pierre Maltais; Pierre, Hanako Nishikawa. [Come in, come in, I'll introduce you. (*He opens the doors to reveal **Hanako** standing behind a low table before the kimono.*)

Hanako, I'd like to introduce you to Pierre Maltais. Pierre, Hanako Nishikawa.]

Pierre   Bonsoir. [Good evening.]

Hanako   Bonsoir . . . (. . .) C'est le fils de Sophie, c'est incroyable! Venez, entrez, vous devez être fatigué . . . [Hello . . . (*She touches his face.*) Sophie's son, it's amazing! Come, come in, you must be tired.]

Pierre   Un peu, oui . . . [A little, yes.]

Hanako   Vous voulez boire quelque chose? Je vais faire du thé. [Would you like something to drink? I'm going to make some tea.]

She exits, feeling her way out along tables and walls. **Pierre** *walks in uncertainly.* **Walter** *looks down at* **Pierre**'*s feet.*

Walter   Pierre, tes souliers . . . [Pierre, your shoes . . .]

Pierre   Oh . . .

He goes onto the porch, kicks off his shoes, and tries to move a hole in one of his socks to the bottom of his foot. **Hanako** *re-enters with a tray of tea. She sits down at the table and pours. There is a silence.* **Pierre***, embarrassed, talks nervously.*

Pierre   J'aimerais m'excuser pour le retard, c'est que j'ai eu des problèmes à Chicago . . . l'avion était plein, ça fait que j'ai été obligé d'en prendre un autre, deux heures plus tard . . . En fait, c'est que j'ai dû changer de compagnie aérienne . . . il a fallu que je prenne mes bagages et que je les enregistre une autre fois . . . (. . .) J'ai la colonne vertébrale comme une tasse de camping, vous savez les petites tasses de plastique qu'on écrase. (. . .) Je suis vraiment désolé . . . [I really have to apologize for being so late; I had problems in Chicago. The plane was full; I had to wait for another, two hours later . . . so I had to take a different airline, which meant I had to get my luggage back and check it in again . . . (*Pause. He takes off his backpack.*) My spine feels like a plastic camping cup. You know, those little plastic cups that you can fold up. (*He gestures crunching a cup. Another pause.*) I am really sorry . . .]

Walter   Pierre, excuse-moi, je voudrais pas te bousculer mais je suis un peu pressé . . . alors si tu permets . . . [Pardon me, Pierre, I don't want to rush you, but I'm pressed for time . . . so if you don't mind . . .]

Walter *puts his briefcase on the table and takes out some papers.*

Walter   Alors, tu avais raison, Hanako, j'ai trouvé des formulaires à l'ambassade pour les étudiants et artistes étrangers en résidence. Je l'ai rempli avec les renseignements que tu m'avais donnés au téléphone. Tout y est. Il ne manque plus que vos deux signatures. Hanako, toi, j'aimerais que tu signes ici. [So, you were right, Hanako. I found the forms at the embassy for renting rooms to foreign students and artists. I filled them out with all the details you gave me on the phone. All that's missing is your two signatures. Hanako, please sign here.]

He puts a form down in front of **Hanako** *and helps her sign it.*

Hanako   Tu pourrais me faire signer n'importe quoi . . . [You could fool me into signing anything . . .]

Walter   (. . .) Toi Pierre, tu n'as qu'à signer en-dessous. [(*Gives the form and pen to* **Pierre**.) Here, Pierre, you just need to sign below her.]

Pierre *is about to sign but stops, surprised.*

Pierre   Y a une erreur ici . . . c'est écrit 500 dollars US par mois . . . [There's a mistake here. It says $500 US a month.]

Walter   C'est ça qui était convenu? [Wasn't that what was agreed on?]

Pierre   Ah non . . . C'était 500 dollars canadiens. [Oh, no, it was $500 Canadian.]

Walter   C'est $500 US, Pierre. [It's $500 US, Pierre.]

Pierre   500 US par mois? Mon budget est déjà très serré. Non vraiment je peux pas me permettre ça . . . Vous comprenez, il faut que je paye mon stage tous les mois. Je sais pas . . . peut-être qu'on peut s'entendre pour 400 dollars US? [$500 US a month! My budget is already tight. No, I really can't manage that. You know, I have to pay for my classes every month. I don't know . . . perhaps you might consider $400 US?]

Walter   Le coût de la vie est très élevé au Japon . . . Avoir su, je t'aurais cherché un ryokan bon marché. [The cost of living is high in Japan. If I had known before, I would have tried to find you an inexpensive ryokan.]

Hanako   (. . .) Ça va aller. 400 dollars US par mois. [(*She touches* **Walter***'s arm*.) It will be fine, $400 US per month.]

Walter   T'es certaine? [You're sure?]

Hanako   Oui, oui, oui . . . [Yes, yes, yes . . .]

Pierre   Je suis désolé, j'ai été un peu surpris. [I'm sorry, I was a little surprised.]

Walter   Bon . . . Veuillez m'excuser, mais il faut vraiment que j'y aille. [Good . . . excuse me, but I really have to go.]

Pierre   Merci beaucoup pour tout, Walter. [Thank you for everything, Walter.]

Walter   Bon séjour au Japon, Pierre! [Have a good stay in Japan, Pierre.]

Pierre *and* **Walter** *shake hands, and* **Walter** *and* **Hanako** *go out onto the porch.*

Walter   Hanako, je te laisse régler les derniers détails. [Hanako, I'll leave you to work out the details.]

As they talk on the porch, **Pierre** *falls asleep.*

Hanako   Je te remercie beaucoup Walter, ça a été très utile, ton aide . . . [Thank you so much, Walter. You have been a great help.]

Walter   Ça m'a fait vraiment plaisir . . . [It's really a pleasure.]

Hanako   Comment va Patricia? Je n'ai pas eu de nouvelles d'elle depuis votre divorce. [How is Patricia doing? I haven't had any news of her since your divorce.]

Walter   Moi non plus je n'ai pas de nouvelles. Je sais seulement qu'elle est retournée à Paris. [I haven't had any news either. All I know is that she returned to Paris.]

Hanako   C'est triste. Tu dois te sentir vraiment seul. [That's sad. You must be lonely.]

Walter   Non, non, non, ça va . . . c'est toi qui dois te sentir seule. Je suis inquiet pour toi, Hanako, depuis que ton mari est décédé. Pourquoi tu viendrais pas passer quelques jours avec moi à Tokyo? [No, it's OK. It's you who must feel lonely. I have been worried about you, Hanako, since your husband died. Why don't you spend a few days with me in Tokyo?]

Hanako   . . . C'est très gentil à toi, mais, j'ai du travail à faire pour un livre que je dois publier bientôt, et puis maintenant que Pierre est ici, je ne serai pas seule . . . Ah mais j'y pense, tiens, je donne une réception pour célébrer mon anniversaire, le mois prochain . . . Je vais fêter mes soixante ans. J'aimerais bien que tu sois là. Je t'invite . . . [You're very kind, but I have work to do on a book I'm going to publish soon, and now that Pierre is here, I won't be alone . . . But, now that I think of it, I'm going to have a party next month to celebrate my birthday. I'm going to be sixty. I would love it if you could come.]

Walter   Ça va me faire plaisir . . . Écoute, il faut vraiment que j'y aille. [I'd love to come. Listen, I really have to go.]

Hanako   Merci encore pour tout. [Thanks again for everything.]

Walter   (. . .) Oh . . . Je crois qu'on a perdu un joueur . . . [(*He sees* **Pierre** *sleeping*.) I think we lost a player.]

Hanako   Il s'est endormi? [Is he asleep?]

Walter   Si tu as des problèmes avec lui, appelle-moi au bureau. (. . .) Prends soin de toi. [If you have any problems with him, call me at the office. (*He kisses her goodbye*.) Take care of yourself.]

Hanako   Ne t'inquiète pas. [Don't worry.]

Walter *leaves.* **Hanako** *goes back into the house and gathers up the tea set.*

2: La chambre/The room

Hanako, *clearing up the teacups, accidentally wakes* **Pierre**.

Pierre   Oh! oh! je suis désolé . . . Où est Walter? [Oh! I'm sorry. Where is Walter?]

Hanako   Walter, il est parti . . . Vous êtes fatigué. [He's gone. You're tired.]

Pierre   Oh! oui . . . [Oh, yes . . .]

Hanako   Venez, je vais vous montrer votre chambre. [Come, I'll show you your room.]

Pierre *gets up and pauses a moment looking at the kimono.* **Hanako** *starts to close the panels.* **Pierre** *grabs his bags and rushes out onto the porch. He picks up his shoes.* **Hanako** *leads him to the stage right door and slides it open to reveal a room the size of two tatami mats, with a futon folded in the corner.*

Hanako   Voilà . . . C'est ici. [Here it is.]

Pierre *stops short in front of his room. Surprised, he drops his shoes.*

Pierre   C'est tout? [That's it?]

Hanako   Oui . . . Deux tatamis. [Yes . . . Two tatamis.]

Pierre   Excusez-moi . . . je comprends pas très bien. [Sorry, I don't understand very well.]

Hanako   Deux tatamis . . . (. . .) Un . . . et deux. [Two tatamis. (*She goes into the room and indicates with her feet.*) One . . . two.]

Pierre   C'est ça deux tatamis! Oh! je croyais que c'était deux chambres avec tatami. [That's two tatamis! I thought it meant two rooms with tatamis!]

Hanako   Deux chambres? Non, non. C'est une chambre avec deux tatamis . . . Ça ne vous plaît pas? [Two rooms? No, no. It's one room with two tatamis . . . You don't like it?]

Pierre   Ah! non, non, non. Euh . . . oui, oui, oui, oui! C'est
. . . intime. [Oh, no, no, no, uh, yes, yes, yes! It's . . .
intimate!]

Hanako   Bon . . . Je vous laisse dormir. Bonne nuit, à
demain. [Good . . . I'll leave you to sleep. Good night; see
you tomorrow.]

Pierre   Bonne nuit. [Good night.]

Hanako *goes back to her room.* **Pierre** *puts his bags in his room and
puts sheets on his futon. Sounds of thunder are heard.* **Pierre** *tries to
close his doors and has trouble making them work. Finally, he slides
them shut. A gong sounds, and a 'ki' – two wooden blocks clacked
together. Blackout.*

*Blue lights shine down the roof of the house, and dim light comes up on
the front of the house. More thunder sounds, and it starts to rain.*
Hanako, *without her sunglasses on, comes out of her bedroom. As she
walks haltingly on the porch, feeling the rain with her hand, she bumps
into* **Pierre***'s shoes. She moves them out of the rain, carefully placing
them side by side in front of* **Pierre***'s room. Following a sudden
impulse, she catches some rainwater with her hand and sensually
splashes her face. She then returns to her room. Ki. Blackout.*

3: Le rêve 1/Dream 1

*The lights come up behind the center panels. Dreamy Japanese music
plays. The kimono seems to come to life: it moves from the frame, turns
around, and moves towards the doors. Now we can see it's* **Nozomi** *in
the kimono. She puts her hands up as if to touch the doors. Blackout.*

4: Arrivée de David/David's arrival

Projection: 'ONE MONTH LATER'.

Lights up in front of the house. **David,** *a young man in a leather suit,
enters, carrying a large tote bag. He is played by the same actor who
played* **Jeffrey 2***. He calls out.*

David   Hanako! . . . Hanako . . . ?

Pierre, *still sleepy, comes out of his room wrapped in a sheet.*

Pierre   Bonjour. Vous voulez parler à Hanako? Sa chambre est juste au bout, là-bas (. . .) Hanako? Hanako? (. . .) Oh! pardon . . . Y'a quelqu'un qui voudrait vous voir. [Hello. You want to talk to Hanako? Her room is at the other end. (*He knocks on* **Hanako**'s *door.*) Hanako? Hanako? (*No answer. He slides her door open and stops quickly.*) Oh! Sorry, there's someone who wants to see you.]

He returns to his room. **Hanako** *comes out of her room.*

David   Bonjour maman. [Hello, Mom.]

Hanako   (. . .) C'est David!!! Tu m'avais dit que tu ne viendrais pas pour mon anniversaire. [(*Throwing her arms around him.*) It's David! You told me you couldn't come for my birthday!]

David   J'ai pu me libérer. [I was able to get free.]

Hanako   C'est formidable! C'est vraiment une surprise fantastique! [This is wonderful. It's truly a fantastic surprise!]

David   Comment vas-tu? [How are you?]

Hanako   Ça va. Tu arrives de Paris? [I'm fine – you've just come from Paris?]

David   Oui, à l'instant. [Yes, just now.]

Hanako   Tu dois être fatigué. Tu dois avoir faim. Je vais préparer quelque chose à manger et puis on va s'asseoir dehors. [You must be tired. You must be hungry. I will make something to eat and we'll sit outside.]

She goes into the house. **David** *speaks to her from outside.*

David   Je savais pas que tu avais déjà des invités. [I didn't know you already had guests.]

Hanako   C'est pas un invité, c'est un locataire. J'ai loué le studio de ton père. [He's not a guest, he's a boarder. I rented your father's studio.]

The next lines are spoken in Japanese.

David   Oka-san, naze oto-san no heya wo kashita no?
[Why did you rent papa's studio?]

Hanako   Okane ga iluno yo. [I needed some money.]

David   Do-shite oshiete kulenakattano? Boku ga yo-date te
agelale tanoni. Boku wa anata no musuko dayo. [Why didn't
you talk to me about this? I have money. I could have given
you some. I'm your son!]

Hanako   Tayoli taku naino. Oto-san ni au mae wa jibun de
yalikuli shiteitano dakala. [I don't want to become
dependent. Before I met your father, I took care of
everything by myself.]

*Hanako comes back outside with a towel, which she gives to **David**.
She gestures to the rain water on the porch.*

Hanako   Tiens . . . Essuie une peu par terre qu'on puisse
s'asseoir. [Here, wipe up a little bit so that we can sit down.]

Pierre, *now dressed, comes out of his room.*

Hanako   Ah, Pierre!

Pierre   Bonjour Hanako. [Hello, Hanako.]

Hanako   Venez que je vous présente mon fils. David, je te
présente Pierre Maltais. Il étudie la danse et il est canadien.
C'est mon fils David, il a une maison de production de
publicité à Paris. Il est probablement le plus jeune
producteur de France . . . Il a vingt-sept ans. Vous, Pierre,
vous avez vingt-six . . . [I'd like you to meet my son. David,
this is Pierre Maltais. He is studying dance and he's
Canadian. This is my son, David. He has an advertising
production company in Paris. He's probably the youngest
producer in France. He's twenty-seven. Pierre, you're
twenty-six, aren't you?]

Pierre   Oui, c'est ça. [Yes, that's right.]

Hanako   C'est proche! Vous allez rester avec nous boire
quelque chose? [That's close . . . will you stay and have
something to drink with us?]

Pierre Je ne veux pas vous déranger. [I don't want to disturb you.]

Hanako Non, non . . . Ça nous fait plaisir. [No, it's our pleasure.]

She goes back inside. Awkward pause. **Pierre** *sits down at the edge of the porch — right in the spot that* **David** *has already dried.* **David** *gives him an irritated look, wipes off another spot a few yards from* **Pierre**, *and sits down. Spotlights come up on them. Another pause.*

David Tu étudies la danse? [You're studying dance?]

Pierre Oui. [Yes.]

David La danse classique, la danse moderne? [Classical dance, modern dance?]

Pierre Le butoh. [Butoh dance.]

David Le butoh? [Butoh?]

Pierre Le butoh, oui. [Yes, butoh.]

David Dis-moi, tu paies combien pour la chambre? [Tell me, how much are you paying for the room?]

Pierre $400 US par mois. [$400 US per month.]

David C'est ridicule! [That's ridiculous!]

Pierre Oui, c'est cher. [Yes, it's expensive.]

David Cher? Tu devrais payer le double! [Expensive? You should be paying double!]

Pierre (. . .) Tu es venu à Hiroshima pour la fête de ta mère? [(*Pause.*) Are you in Hiroshima for your mother's party?]

David Oui . . . Je voulais passer quelque temps seul avec elle, mais maintenant . . . avec les amis, les invités et les nouveaux locataires, ça commence à faire beaucoup de monde . . . [Yes, I wanted to spend some time alone with her, but now with friends, guests, and new borders, it's starting to get a little crowded.]

Hanako *comes back out.*

Hanako   Vous allez prendre du thé vert ou du thé noir?
[Do you want green tea or black tea?]

David   Non, moi maman, je vais aller au ryokan. [No, mom, I'm going to go to a ryokan.]

He gets up and prepares to leave.

Hanako   (. . .) Au ryokan? Non non non! Mon fils à l'hôtel! . . . Écoute, y'a de la place, on va s'arranger. [(*She stops him.*) My son at a hotel? Never! Listen, there's enough room, we'll work it out.]

Pierre   Écoutez, vous pouvez prendre ma chambre, je vais dormir dans le salon . . . [Listen, you can take my room; I'll sleep in the living room.]

Hanako   Non, non, Pierre, vous, vous payez pour la chambre, vous allez dormir dans la chambre. David va dormir avec moi. (. . .) Il ne veut pas coucher avec sa mère . . . Allez, viens, on va arranger quelque chose . . . [No, Pierre, you're paying for the room, you'll sleep in the room. David will sleep in my bed. (**David** *doesn't move.*) He doesn't want to sleep with his mother. Come on, we'll work something out.]

*She goes into her room, with **David** following. **Pierre** is still sitting on the porch. **Hanako** comes back out.*

Hanako   Pierre, vous voulez boire du thé vert ou noir? [Pierre, would you like green tea or black tea?]

Pierre   Noir. [Black.]

5: Butoh

*Ki. The lights go off on the porch and come up on the rock garden. Live, loud, percussive Japanese music plays. **Pierre** jumps off the step into the rock garden, and starts to perform butoh exercises, crossing up and down the rock garden. The movements are athletic, rigorous, yet graceful. After a few minutes of dancing, he starts to falter, then collapses onto the step in exhaustion. The lights go down on the garden.*

6: Fête d'Hanako/Hanako's party

Piano music plays. Lights up inside the house and dim lights up on the porch, illuminating a line of shoes which has appeared along the threshhold. **Hanako** *slides open the doors to reveal a group of people —* **David** *and* **Jana** *among them — sitting with their backs to the audience facing* **Ada,** *who stands with sheet music in her hand.*

Hanako   Walter! Walter! Ada va chanter. [Walter! Walter! Ada is going to sing!]

Walter *doesn't appear.*

Ada (*sings Dvořák's 'Gipsy Song', in Czech*)
'Often, when teaching me to sing,
my mother's eyes filled with tears.
And now, as I teach the children to play and sing,
tears run down my own brown cheek.'

She sings the same song in Japanese. As she sings, **Pierre** *enters and tiptoes across the open doors to his room. He stands and listens a bit, then opens his door.* **Walter** *is in* **Pierre**'*s room, in bed with a young Japanese woman.* **Pierre** *quickly shuts the door and backs away, startled. The door opens and the girl scurries across the porch.* **Walter** *follows her and disappears after her, calling:*

Walter   Masako! Masako!

David *hears the noise and stands up to shut the doors. He shushes* **Pierre** *as he does so.* **Pierre** *enters his room, and takes the sheets off his bed.* **Walter** *comes back and lights a cigarette.* **Ada**'*s singing ends.*

Ada (*in English*)   Happy birthday, Hanako!

Applause inside.

Walter   (. . .) Excuse-moi, Pierre, je peux te parler deux minutes? [(*He looks embarrassed.*) Excuse me, Pierre, could I talk to you for a few minutes?]

Pierre   Ça va, c'est correct, je comprends. [That's OK, I understand.]

Walter J'insiste, Pierre, viens, suis moi. (. . .) Écoute
Pierre, ce qui vient de se passer, j'aimerais que ça reste entre
nous deux. Tu vois, Masako est mineure. C'est la nièce
d'Hanako. Je voudrais pas la blesser pour rien, tu
comprends? [I insist, Pierre, come here. Follow me. (**Pierre**
comes out and sits on the edge of the porch.) I'd really appreciate it if
what you saw stayed between us. Masako is a minor and she's
Hanako's niece. I wouldn't want to hurt her for anything,
you do understand?]

Pierre Non, pas vraiment. Qu'est-ce que vous voulez dire
au juste? [No, not really. What are you trying to say?]

Walter Voyons Pierre . . . T'as des amis? J'veux dire, des
vrais amis. [Look, Pierre. You have friends, real friends?]

Pierre Oui . . . [Yes.]

Walter Est-ce que tu dis toujours tout à tes amis? [Do you
always tell your friends everything?]

Pierre Oui. [Yes.]

Walter En tous cas . . . Ne pas tout dire, ce n'est pas
nécessairement mentir . . . (. . .) Tu dois te sentir bien seul
ici. [Anyway . . . Not telling everything isn't necessarily
lying . . . (*Pause.*) You must feel lonely here.]

Pierre Oui. [Yes.]

Walter Si tu veux, je pourrais te présenter quelqu'un . . .
[If you want, I could introduce you to someone.]

Pierre Non, merci. [No, thank you.]

Jana *slides one of the doors open.*

Jana (*in English*)   Walter? It's time for the cake . . .

Walter Oui oui, j'arrive tout de suite! (. . .) Tu viens,
Pierre? [Yes, yes, I'm coming! (*Inside,* **Hanako** *is brought a
birthday cake, and the guests sing 'Happy Birthday', in French and
English.*) Are you coming, Pierre?]

Pierre   Non merci, c'est pas vraiment ma place, et puis de toute façon, je connais personne. [No, thank you, I'd be out of place, and besides, I don't know anyone.]

Walter   C'est une excellente occasion de rencontrer des gens, non? [It's an excellent opportunity to meet people, isn't it?]

He opens the door and ushers **Pierre** *in, who resists.*

Pierre   Non, Walter, non, non, Walter, s'il-vous-plaît! [No, Walter, no, no, Walter, please!]

Walter   Hanako, j'ai une surprise pour toi! [Hanako, I have a surprise for you!]

Hanako   Encore! Ah, qu'est-ce que c'est? [Another one! What is it?]

Pierre *has lost the struggle; he and* **Walter** *go in to the living room.*

Jana (*in English*)   It's a handsome young man!

Hanako   Ah! C'est Pierre! Allez, entrez. [Ah, it's Pierre! Come in!]

Ki. Blackout.

7: Le rêve 2/Dream 2

Lights up behind the screens. **Nozomi** *and* **Luke** *appear in silhouette in a sexual embrace. They lie down as they start to make love. A male figure rises from where they lay, but it's* **Pierre**, *not* **Luke**. *Blackout.*

8: Départ de David/David's departure

Projection: 'THE NEXT DAY'.

Lights up on the porch. **Hanako** *rushes out of her room, wearing a silk robe. She calls out urgently.*

Hanako   David! David!

She opens the door to the living room, then shuts it, and heads towards **Pierre**'s *room.* **Pierre** *slides his door open halfway and peeks out. He's wearing only his underwear.*

Pierre   Hanako . . . Qu'est-ce qui se passe? [Hanako, what's going on?]

Hanako   David doit prendre le train à dix heures, je ne me suis pas réveillée . . . Il va être en retard. [David needs to catch a train at 10 a.m., but I just woke up. He's going to be late.]

Pierre   Il est quelle heure? [What time is it?]

Hanako   Neuf heures. Vous ne l'avez pas vu? [It's nine o'clock. You haven't seen him?]

Pierre   Non. [No.]

David *appears behind* **Pierre** *in his room, also wearing only underwear.*

Hanako   Si vous le voyez, dites lui qu'il va rater son train. [If you see him, tell him he's going to miss his train.]

She goes back to her room. **Pierre** *hands* **David**'s *clothes to him.* **David** *leaves* **Pierre**'s *room, then, pretending he went jogging, he runs noisily to his mother's room, and stops, panting.*

David   Bonjour. [Good morning.]

Hanako   T'as fait la course? [You went running?]

David   Oui, j'ai couru . . . [Yes, I ran.]

Hanako   Dépêche-toi, tu vas rater ton train. Il est déjà neuf heures. [Hurry up, you're going to miss your train. It's already nine o'clock.]

David   Ah merde! [Oh shit!]

Hanako   J'ai commencé à faire ta valise, j'espère que je n'ai rien oublié. (. . .) J'ai mis dans ton sac les deux bouteilles de saké que ta tante a apporté. [I've started to pack your suitcase. I hope I haven't forgotten anything. (**David** *goes into her room.*) I put those two bottles of sake your aunt brought in your bag.]

David   C'est gentil, merci. [That's nice, thank you.]

Hanako   Est-ce que tu as bien choisi les photos dans l'album de famille? [Did you choose pictures from the family album?]

David   Oui. J'ai fait ça hier soir. [Yes. I did it last night.]

Hanako   Tu les as prises avec toi? [You've taken them with you?]

David   Oui. [Yes.]

Hanako   Tu vas rester quelques jours à Tokyo? [You're going to spend a few days in Tokyo?]

David   Oui, quatre jours. [Yes, four days.]

Hanako   Écoute, y a Monsieur Tanaka qui m'a dit: 'Quand David passera par Tokyo, vous pouvez lui demander de me téléphoner s'il-vous-plaît?' Je crois qu'il a des musiques qu'il aimerait te faire entendre dans son studio. [Listen, Mr Tanaka said to me, 'When David passes through Tokyo, could you have him call me, please?' I think he has some music he wants you to listen to in his studio.]

David   Maman, tu sais que je déteste ce qu'il fait! [Mother, you know I hate what he does.]

Hanako   Tu n'as qu'à faire semblant d'aimer ça. Ça me fait plaisir et puis ça lui fait plaisir aussi. [Pretend that you like it. It'll give me pleasure and make him happy.]

David   Bon, d'accord . . . J'irai . . . [All right, I'll go . . .]

Hanako   Tu seras à Paris samedi? [You're going to be in Paris Saturday?]

David   Oui, j'arrive samedi. [Yes, I'm arriving Saturday.]

Hanako   Tu vas me téléphoner quand tu arriveras là-bas? [Will you call me when you get there?]

David   Bien sûr. [Of course.]

Pierre *comes out of his room, dressed and carrying a rucksack.*

Pierre   Bonne journée, Hanako. [Have a good day, Hanako.]

Hanako   Bonne journée, Pierre. [Have a good day, Pierre.]

David *comes out of* **Hanako**'s *room, dressed.*

Pierre   Au revoir David. Bon retour à Paris! [Bye, David. Have a good trip to Paris!]

Hanako *goes into the house.*

David   Tu pars maintenant? [You're leaving now?]

Pierre   Oui, j'ai un rendez-vous, je suis déjà très en retard. [Yes, I'm meeting someone, I'm already really late.]

David   Écoute, je dois me rendre à la gare, on peut peut-être marcher ensemble . . . [Well, listen, I'm going to the station. Maybe we could walk together?]

Pierre   Non, vraiment, je suis très en retard. [No, really, I'm very late.]

David   On peut prendre un taxi, je peux te déposer là-bas. [We could take a taxi; I could drop you.]

Pierre   Non, non . . . Je crois que c'est beaucoup plus rapide à pied . . . Au revoir. Bon voyage . . . [No, I think it'll be much faster on foot. Goodbye. Have a good trip.]

He kisses **David** *on both cheeks and exits.* **David** *watches him go, then sits on the threshold to put his shoes on. He talks to* **Hanako** *who is still offstage.*

David   Tu sais, maman, hier il faisait trop chaud, j'ai préféré dormir au salon, c'était plus frais . . . [Listen, Mom, I didn't sleep with you last night because it was too hot. I slept in the living room; it's cooler there.]

Hanako *comes out onto the porch.*

Hanako   Oui, oui . . . Je suis peut-être aveugle, mais je ne suis pas sourde. [Yes . . . I may be blind, but I'm not deaf.]

David *does a take, then busies himself getting his things together sheepishly.*

Hanako   (. . .) Allez, dépêche-toi, tu vas rater ton train,
dépêche-toi, tu es déjà en retard, va-t'en . . . Tu vas me
téléphoner? Tu vas me manquer . . . [(**Hanako** *smiles to
herself.*) Come on, hurry up, you're going to miss your train.
You're already late. Call me. I'm going to miss you . . .]

David *hugs her and leaves. Pause. She goes inside, comes back with a
small basket, and sits down on the edge of the porch.*

9: Le jardin/The garden

Slow, dreamlike Japanese music plays. **Hanako** *puts on make-up –
powder, then lipstick, then slowly reaches inside her blouse and caresses
her breasts.*

Ki. The light changes, as if the whole day had passed. **Hanako** *is now
sitting with her hands on her lap.* **Pierre** *enters in slow motion,
carrying a bouquet of flowers. The light goes through the flowers,
creating a strange and dreamlike atmosphere. Ki. Back to normal.*

Pierre   Bonsoir, Hanako. [Good evening, Hanako.]

Hanako   Pierre. (. . .) Ça sent bon. Vous avez acheté des
fleurs? [Pierre. (*He walks towards her room. She smells the air.*)
That smells good. You bought some flowers?]

Pierre   (. . .) Oui . . . Je voulais vous faire une surprise
. . . Je suis un peu en retard mais. (. . .) Joyeux anniversaire.
[(*Surprised.*) Yes, I wanted to surprise you. I'm a little bit
late, but . . . (*He gives them to her.*) Happy birthday.]

Hanako   Ah merci. Merci, c'est vraiment gentil. (. . .) Ce
sont des lys . . . [Thank you, thank you, that's truly kind.
(*She touches the flowers.*) These are lilies . . .]

Pierre   Oui, c'est ça. [Yes, you're right.]

Hanako   Des fresias. [And freesias . . .]

Pierre   Vous connaissez bien les fleurs? [You know flowers
well?]

Hanako   Un peu. Vous savez, il y a plusieurs années,
quand nous sommes revenus de Paris mon mari a fait un

jardin devant la maison, et je l'ai aidé un peu . . . [A little.
You know, years ago, when we came back here from Paris,
my husband decided to plant a garden in front of the house
and I helped him a bit.]

Pierre　Qu'est-ce que vous aviez planté? [What did you
grow?]

As **Hanako** *describes the garden, she stands up and moves haltingly
around the rock garden, illustrating her descriptions with gestures.*
Pierre *moves to the porch and watches her closely, discreetly
mirroring her movements. The slow Japanese music continues.*

Hanako　Ici, il y avait des bosquets de pivoines, qui
couvraient toute la surface, c'étaient vraiment des fleurs
énormes. (. . .) Un jour, mon mari, qui était musicien, avait
fait une tournée en Italie, et, de là, il avait ramené des dalles
de marbre très fin et avec ça, on avait fait une petite allée et
on pouvait marcher à travers les arbustes. Le long des
marches, il y avait des petits cèdres qu'il avait fait venir
d'Amérique . . . Et par là, il avait creusé un bassin assez
grand . . . Il y avait des poissons, des plantes aquatiques, des
algues aussi, des nénuphars. Un jour, il a fallu construire une
clôture, parce que le voisin avait un petit chien qui venait
faire pipi et ça faisait mourir les plantes. (. . .) Et là il y avait
un arbre immense qui devait être très vieux; il devait avoir
au moins cinquante ans, un saule pleureur, avec des branches
qui tombaient comme ça . . . (. . .) Mais les racines
poussaient très vite . . .Elles étaient trop puissantes et elle
menaçaient de détruire les fondations de la maison. Alors il a
fallu l'arracher. (. . .) Après la mort de mon mari, David est
retourné vivre à Paris alors, comme je ne pouvais pas faire
l'entretien du jardin toute seule, on a tout enlevé et j'ai fait
mettre des pierres à la place. (. . .) Vous entendez ça? [Here,
there was a grove of peonies, that covered the ground, really
huge flowers. (*She moves further, thinks a moment.*) One day, my
husband, who was a musician, did a tour in Italy, and he
brought back some fine marble paving stones and made a
little walking path so we could walk in between the hedges.
Here, along the walk, there were some little cedars that he

brought from America . . . And here, he dug a big pond. We had fish, aquatic plants, seaweed too, water lilies . . . one day, he had to build a fence, because the neighbor had a little dog that would pee on the plants, and it was killing them. (*She suddenly stops and seems very moved.*) And here, there was a huge, old tree; it must have been fifty years old, a weeping willow, with branches that leaned over like this . . . (*She slowly raises her arms in the air as if to demonstrate.*) But the roots grew too fast and they threatened the foundation so we had to cut it down. (*She indicates that she wants to sit.* **Pierre** *helps her.*) After my husband died, David went back to Paris, and I couldn't keep up the garden, so we pulled out the flowers and put stones in their place. (*Pause. We hear the sound of a river flowing.*) Do you hear that?]

Pierre   Oui. [Yes.]

Hanako   C'est la rivière. Ce que j'aime de cette maison, c'est qu'elle est située juste à l'endroit où la rivière Ota se divise en sept parties. (. . .) Je vais rentrer. (. . .) Merci pour les fleurs, c'est très délicat. (. . .) Ah, j'allais oublier . . . Votre mère a téléphoné aujourd'hui. Le spectacle dans lequel elle devait jouer à Montréal a été annulé. Alors maintenant, elle est libre. Elle va venir nous visiter; elle sera là la semaine prochaine. J'ai bien hâte de la revoir. Bonne nuit. [It's the river. What I love about this house is that it's located right where the River Ota divides into seven streams. (*Pause.*) I should go inside. (*He helps her to her doorway.*) Thank you for the flowers; that was very thoughtful. (*Pause.*) Oh, I almost forgot. Your mother called today. The show she was going to do in Montreal was cancelled, so she's free. She's going to come visit us next week. I can't wait to see her.]

Pierre   Ah bon . . . [Really!]

Hanako *goes into her room.* **Pierre,** *in a pensive mood, slowly moves towards his room, imitating some of* **Hanako**'s *hand gestures as he goes, and shuts the door behind him. Blackout. Ki.*

10: Le Musée de la Paix/The Peace Museum

When the lights come up, the doors are all open to reveal a room in the Hiroshima Peace Museum, in which models of three bombed buildings, including the A-Bomb Dome, are displayed. Large photographs of the mushroom cloud and of bomb damage are projected on the back wall. **Sophie,** *young and still pregnant, enters, and recites a passage from Mishima's* Five Modern No Plays. *She speaks in French, which is translated into supertitles. The passage she recites is a first-person account of a horrible explosion; the speaker's memory is tormented with visions of death and destruction. Though the passage does not state it outright, it is clear that the speaker is talking about the bombing of Hiroshima or Nagasaki. At the end of the passage, she identifies the author and title of the work.*

The dresser from 'Words' enters and helps **Sophie** *transform into her present-day self:* **Sophie** *takes off her '70s wig and the minidress that makes her look pregnant and puts on a contemporary wig and a trouser suit. She is then joined by* **Pierre,** *and together they look at the exhibition.* **Ada** *and* **Walter** *enter together.* **Sophie** *notices and approaches them.*

Sophie   Walter Lapointe? (. . .) Vous me reconnaissez pas? [Walter Lapointe? (*Pause.*) You don't remember me?]

Walter   (. . .) . . . Non. [(*He looks at her embarrassedly.*) . . . No.]

Sophie   Sophie Maltais?

Walter   Non, je suis désolé . . . [No, I'm sorry . . .]

Sophie   (. . .) C'est La Môme Crevette, parbleu! [(*In her Feydeau character voice:*) It's the Shrimp Kid, zounds!]

Walter *recognizes her and shakes her hand.*

Sophie   Comment allez-vous? Toujours au Japon? [How are you? Still in Japan?]

Walter   Oui, oui. [Yes, yes.]

Sophie   Je suis venue visiter mon fils. (. . .) C'est mon grand garçon, Pierre. [I'm here to visit my son. (*She ushers* **Pierre** *over to meet* **Walter**.) This is my big boy, Pierre.]

Walter *and* **Pierre** *recognize each other, and shake hands.*

Walter   (. . .) C'est votre fils? On se connait. C'est moi qui lui a fait signer son bail. [(*To* **Sophie**.) This is your son? We know each other. I helped him sign his lease.]

Pierre   (. . .) Vous vous connaissez? [(*To* **Sophie**.) You know each other?]

Sophie   (. . .) Ah, c'est une longue histoire . . . On s'est connu il y a vingt-cinq ans, quand j'étais à Osaka pour jouer un Feydeau à l'expo universelle. Un grand moment de théâtre! [(*To* **Pierre**.) It's a long story . . . we met twenty-five years ago when I was in Osaka to play a Feydeau at the Universal Expo. A great moment of theater!] (*She laughs and so does* **Ada**.)

Walter (*in English*)   Oh, I'm sorry . . . let me introduce you to Ada Weber.

They shake hands.

Sophie   Nice to meet you. I saw you sing in New York last winter. It was beautiful.

Ada   Thank you. Hanako has told me a lot about you . . . because of Pierre. (*Uncomfortable pause.*)

Sophie   Bon, bien . . . on doit y aller; ça m'a fait plaisir de vous revoir. (. . .) À la prochaine. Dans vingt ans, peut-être? [Oh, good . . . we should go. It was a pleasure to meet you. (*To* **Walter**.) See you again. In twenty years, maybe!]

Walter   Pierre, écoute, si tu as besoin de quelque chose pendant ton séjour, n'hésite pas à me téléphoner. [Pierre, if you need anything while you're here, don't hesitate to call me.]

Pierre   Merci. [Thank you.]

Pierre *and* **Sophie** *exit.*

Ada (*in English*)   Do you want to go to the little café just across the plaza?

Walter (*he seems to be a bit shaken*)   Yes, I need a good coffee.

They exit.

11: Diapos/Slides

A rectangle of light appears on the stage right side of the porch and moves slowly to center stage, then descends slowly. It is a slide viewer. **David** *and* **Pierre**, *sitting on the porch, both shirtless, put it on their laps and lean over it, looking at pictures.*

Pierre   C'est ton père, ici? [Is this your father?]

David   Oui. [Yes.]

Pierre   Tu lui ressembles. [You look like him.]

David   Physiquement, oui . . . Mais on avait des personnalités très différentes. Tu vois, lui, il était musicien, le genre de mec replié sur lui-même, toujours enfermé dans son studio, les écouteurs sur les oreilles . . . De toute façon, je me suis toujours senti plus près de ma mère. (. . .) Après la mort de mon père, j'ai offert à ma mère de venir habiter avec moi à Paris, mais elle a pas voulu. Alors je lui ai dit: Hanako, tant que tu balanceras pas ses cendres dans la baie d'Hiroshima, tu pourras pas l'oublier! (. . .) Ça l'a vexée, elle m'a pas parlé pendant un an. (. . .) Et toi, tu t'entends bien avec ton père? [Maybe physically, but our personalities were different. You see, he was a musician, the type that was always holed up in his studio, with headphones, withdrawn into himself. Anyway, I always felt much closer to my mother. (*Pause.*) After Father died I asked her to come live with me in Paris, but she didn't want to. I told her, 'Hanako, until you throw Father's ashes in the bay of Hiroshima you will never be able to forget.' She got upset and didn't talk to me for a year. (*Pause.*) And you, do you get along with your father?]

Pierre   Je l'ai jamais connu. [I never knew him.]

They stand up with the slide box in front of them, so that it is impossible to see the action behind it. When the light box descends again, it's **Sophie** *and* **Hanako** *who are holding it on their laps. They are drinking glasses of scotch and are a bit drunk.*

Hanako   Walter?

Sophie   Oui! [Yes!]

Hanako   Walter Lapointe?

Sophie   Oui! [Yes!]

Hanako   Mais est-ce qu'il est au courant? [Does he know?]

Sophie   Non!! (. . .) Et Pierre non plus, d'ailleurs, hein . . .
Écoute, c'était tellement drôle quand je les ai croisés cet
après-midi, au Musée . . . J'te mens pas, j'ai failli le dire!
[No! (*They laugh.*) And, what's more, neither does Pierre. So,
listen, when I saw them in the museum this afternoon. I'm
not kidding – I felt like telling him.]

Hanako   Mais pourquoi tu l'as pas dit? [So why didn't you
say anything?]

Sophie   Parce que . . . il était avec quelqu'un! Tu sais, ta
copine, la chanteuse d'opéra . . . [Because . . . he was there
with someone! You know, your friend, the opera singer.]

Hanako   Ada?

Sophie   Oui! [Yes!]

Hanako   Ada Weber?

Sophie   Oui! J'ai l'impression que . . . (. . .) hmm-hmm-
hmm . . . [Yes! And I had the feeling that they . . . (*She raises
her eyebrows and makes a 'you know what I mean' noise.*) Mm,
hmm . . .]

Hanako   Non! [No!]

Sophie   Alors, tu comprends, c'était vraiment pas le
moment! (. . .) Bon, montre-moi tes photos . . . [So, you
understand, it would have been truly bad timing. (*They
explode into giddy laughter.*) So, show me your pictures.]

She leans over the light box.

Hanako   (. . .) À la maison d'édition, ils ont engagé un
photographe mais je ne le connais pas . . . Il a choisi ces trois
photos. Il a dit que ce sont les meilleures. Je voulais avoir ton
avis . . . [(*She shows* **Sophie** *the pictures, spreading them on the
light box.*) The photographer that the publisher hired took

these pictures, but I don't know him. He said these three were the ones he liked the most, but I want your opinion.]

Sophie   Bon, celle-là, je l'aime pas du tout. T'as pas tes lunettes, ça te ressemble pas. Ces deux-là sont très bien, mais en fait, ça dépend de ce que l'éditeur préfère. Moi, celle que j'aime le mieux, c'est celle où tu souris . . . [This one I don't like; you don't have your sunglasses on. You don't look like yourself at all. These two are good, but it really depends on what the editor wants. I like this one the best, because you're smiling.]

Hanako   Ah bon? [Oh really?]

Sophie   Je la trouve plus sympathique. [I think it's more likeable.]

Hanako   Alors c'est mieux la sympathique . . . [Good, the most likeable one is the best.]

Sophie   Je trouve, vraiment. [I think so, really.]

Hanako   Tu peux la mettre ici? [Can you put it here?] (*She extends her hand.*)

Sophie   Oui. [Yes.] (*She does so.*)

Pierre *enters.*

Sophie   Pierre?

Pierre   Bonsoir. [Good evening.]

Sophie   Bonsoir, chéri. [Good evening, honey.]

Pierre   Bonsoir, Hanako. [Good evening, Hanako.]

Hanako   Bonsoir. [Good evening.]

Sophie   Tu as passé une belle soirée? [Have you had a pleasant evening?]

Pierre   Oui. [Yes.]

Sophie   Ben nous autres aussi . . . [Ours was good too.]

Pierre   Ah bon? [Really?]

Sophie Mais je pense que j'ai un petit peu trop bu, alors je vais aller me coucher, OK? [But I think I had a little bit too much to drink, so I'm going to go to bed, OK?]

Hanako Alors bonne nuit. On va manger ensemble demain matin. [So good night. We'll have breakfast together tomorrow morning.]

Sophie Oui, bonne nuit! [Yes, good night!]

Pierre Bonne nuit. [Good night.]

Sophie *exits.*

12: La danse du kimono/The kimono dance

Hanako Vous voulez un verre de scotch? [Would you like a glass of scotch?]

Pierre Ah oui, s'il-vous-plaît. [Yes, please.]

Hanako Regardez . . . (. . .) J'ai besoin d'une photo pour mon livre et votre mère a choisi celle-la: [Look . . . (*She hands him the slide viewer.*) I need a picture for my book, and your mother chose this one.]

Pierre Vous êtes très belle, Hanako. [You are very beautiful, Hanako.]

Pause.

Hanako Vos leçons de danse, ça s'est bien passé? [Your dance lessons went well?]

She hands him a glass of scotch.

Pierre Oui, très bien. Je suis en train de travailler sur la chorégraphie que je vais présenter la semaine prochaine. [Yes, very well. I'm working on the choreography that I am going to present next week.]

Hanako Qu'est-ce que vous allez faire? [What will you do?]

Pierre J'ai envie de raconter l'histoire d'une femme. [I would like to tell the story of woman.]

Hanako   Une femme . . . [A woman . . .]

Pierre   Oui. Une hibakusha. Une survivante d'Hiroshima
. . . (. . .) Hanako, est-ce que vous avez de la poudre? [Yes.
A hibakusha. A survivor of Hiroshima . . . (*Long pause.*)
Hanako, do you have some powder?]

Hanako   Du maquillage? [Make-up?]

Pierre   Oui. [Yes.]

Hanako *goes inside the house and comes back with her basket of
make-up. She sits beside* **Pierre**.

Hanako   C'est pour votre personnage? [Is it for your
character?]

Pierre   Oui. [Yes.]

Hanako *slowly starts to put make-up on* **Pierre**. *After she has put
lipstick on his lips, she beckons for him to follow her into the house.
Lights come up in the living room.*

Hanako   (. . .) Enlève ça. [(*Softly, touching* **Pierre**'*s T-
shirt.*) Take this off.]

Japanese music plays. **Pierre** *takes off his shirt.* **Hanako** *picks up
the kimono and holds it out for him, turning slowly so that she is no
longer visible behind the kimono. He puts one arm in the kimono and
turns with it. As he turns, the person holding the kimono becomes visible
again, but it is not* **Hanako** *anymore; it's* **older Jana**, *who is
putting the kimono on* **Sarah**. **Jana** *stands back and watches.* **Sarah**
*faces the audience; she is wearing her gray suit under the kimono. She
walks forward slowly, turns, and walks back, her lips moving as
though singing. With her back to the audience, she holds her arms out,
lifts them up so that her head disappears behind the kimono. The
kimono then drops down onto* **Nozomi**'*s shoulders. She is sitting on
the tatamis;* **Luke** *has appeared, standing behind his camera, facing
the audience. He touches her hair, and helps her stand up. He steps back
and takes a picture of her. She raises the kimono up over her head. When
the kimono comes back down, it's* **Pierre** *who's wearing it. At the
same time,* **Luke** *turns around slowly, and* **Hanako** *appears in his
place. She walks to the threshold and sits down.* **Pierre** *turns around
slowly. His make-up shows up strongly under the lights – his face looks*

white. He performs a butoh dance in which a woman moves gracefully, then experiences a moment of terror and pain. When he is finished, **Pierre** *collapses onto the tatamis.* **Hanako** *goes to him and caresses his back. She then walks slowly back into her room. Thunder sounds.* **Pierre** *stands up and takes off the kimono. It starts to rain. He closes the sliding doors, goes to the edge of the porch, captures some water in his hands, and washes the make-up off his face. He heads towards his room, but changes his mind, and goes to* **Hanako**'s *room, opens the door, enters, and shuts it behind him. Ki. Blackout.*

Epilogue: The Torii of Miyajima

The lights come up. **Walter, Ada, Sophie, David** *and* **Hanako** *are standing on a balcony overlooking a torii arch — the torii in the Bay of Miyajima.* **Jana** *stands facing them.* **David** *helps* **Hanako** *walk towards* **Jana***; she gives* **Jana** *an urn.* **Jana** *performs a short ritual over the urn and pours its contents — ashes — into the bay.* **Jana** *exits, and then everyone after her, until* **Hanako** *is left alone on the balcony.* **Pierre** *enters, takes her arm, and they exit together.*

The gagaku music from the prologue plays. The boatman and **Luke** *enter, silhouetted against the sky and the torii. The boatman helps* **Luke** *into the boat and pushes off,* **Luke** *sets up his camera and looks into it. The lights fade out.*

Methuen Modern Plays

include work by

Jean Anouilh
John Arden
Margaretta D'Arcy
Peter Barnes
Sebastian Barry
Brendan Behan
Edward Bond
Bertolt Brecht
Howard Brenton
Simon Burke
Jim Cartwright
Caryl Churchill
Noël Coward
Sarah Daniels
Nick Dear
Shelagh Delaney
David Edgar
Dario Fo
Michael Frayn
John Godber
Paul Godfrey
David Greig
John Guare
Peter Handke
Jonathan Harvey
Iain Heggie
Declan Hughes
Terry Johnson
Sarah Kane
Charlotte Keatley
Barrie Keeffe
Robert Lepage
Stephen Lowe

Doug Lucie
Martin McDonagh
John McGrath
David Mamet
Patrick Marber
Arthur Miller
Mtwa, Ngema & Simon
Tom Murphy
Phyllis Nagy
Peter Nichols
Joseph O'Connor
Joe Orton
Louise Page
Joe Penhall
Luigi Pirandello
Stephen Poliakoff
Franca Rame
Mark Ravenhill
Philip Ridley
Reginald Rose
David Rudkin
Willy Russell
Jean-Paul Sartre
Sam Shepard
Wole Soyinka
C. P. Taylor
Theatre de Complicite
Theatre Workshop
Sue Townsend
Judy Upton
Timberlake Wertenbaker
Victoria Wood

Printed in the United Kingdom
by Lightning Source UK Ltd.
130473UK00001B/27/A